Trauma Survivors' Strategies for Healing

A Workbook to Help You Grow,
Rebuild, and Take Back Your Life

Trauma Survivors' Strategies
—— for ——
Healing

ELENA WELSH, PhD

ALTHEA
PRESS

Dedicated to all the trauma survivors who have bravely shared their stories with me.
You have taught me time and again about the resiliency of the human spirit.

———————

CONTENTS

INTRODUCTION

No human life is untouched by trauma. Whether we experience it directly or witness it from a distance, we've all known trauma in some form or another.

As a psychologist, I've worked with so many people who have lived through unimaginable pain. A woman whose mother sold her for drug money as a young girl. Survivors of government-inflicted torture who had their limbs cut off. Men and women who lived in war zones and were kept awake at night by the sounds of bombs, wondering which one might signal their impending death. I've talked with mothers who have lost their children, sorrow coursing through every bone of their bodies and increasing with every breath. Girls and men who have been brutally raped, sometimes by their own family members, and women who have had their heads slammed against the wall at the hands of their intimate partners. I've worked with people who were so angry that they would hit anyone or anything that came within striking distance.

But within each of these unthinkable tragedies, I have also heard stories of strength, hope, love, reconnection, and growth.

Trauma has touched my life, too. Generations ago, my family lived through the Armenian genocide. More recently, we endured the pain and confusion of a parental suicide. Some of my best friends have been raped or beaten by their intimate partners. The more trauma I encounter—either directly or through my clients and loved ones—the more and more faith I have in the resiliency of the human spirit. I believe that people can endure the unthinkable—and from that pain, they can create something beautiful.

I also believe in science. I believe in its logic and in its ability to support our natural inclinations to heal ourselves (and others). We cannot conquer what we do not understand, and science can tell us whether something that intuitively feels like a good idea will truly help. It can also tell us *why* and *how* it helps. In recent years, science has provided countless insights into how we can heal our minds and spirits. Right now, dedicated researchers are working tirelessly to understand the similarities that span the human experience and the precise mechanisms required to heal from tragedy and trauma.

In addition to working therapeutically with a wide range of trauma survivors and seeing firsthand what helped them heal, I've also spent time studying the way people cope with trauma and identifying which factors are associated with better mental health outcomes. In one research study, I interviewed women who had emigrated from war-torn Afghanistan in order to understand how each woman dealt with the adversity she faced. While everyone responds to trauma in their own way, there are also some commonalities regarding which factors hold people back and what helps them survive—and even thrive. I have also worked on statewide projects with other mental health and trauma specialists in order to examine how institutions, like psychiatric hospitals, can either help trauma survivors heal or further harm them.

The strategies discussed in the following pages have been scientifically proven to work. These exercises have helped thousands of trauma survivors cope with debilitating emotions and experiences and have been shown to reduce (and even eliminate) trauma-related symptoms over time. Through this book, it is my hope to arm you with the tools you need to heal.

A Note to Readers

The names and other identifying information of all clients described in this book have been altered to protect their privacy.

HOW TO USE THIS BOOK

This book was designed to be used in whatever way is most helpful to you. You can begin at the beginning and work your way through in order if you like, but the exercises are grouped by category and are not dependent on being done in sequential order.

As an alternative to working from beginning to end, you can skip to whichever section makes the most sense for you, depending on what you're struggling with most right now. Any step you take on your journey toward healing is an important step to take. That said, every trauma survivor will benefit from *every* chapter and exercise presented here, so if you decide to skip over some sections this time around, plan to circle back at some point and see what the other sections have to teach you.

Many of the workbook quizzes and assessments are meant to be self-diagnostic, to help you identify the specific symptoms you are experiencing and give you some useful, consistent language to describe them. This will provide you with a deeper understanding of what you're dealing with so you can better prioritize your goals, track your progress, and select the most effective strategies and interventions for you.

Typically, exercises and skill building are easier to do when you're calm, able to focus, and not in the throes of a strong emotion or traumatic memory. When you are in a state of crisis or feeling overwhelmed by a memory or emotion, it is not uncommon for your mind to go blank. You may forget what you were working on or feel like everything is too hard. During these moments, I encourage you to return to whatever section or skill you may have found useful before. This will not only provide you with a tangible distraction from your difficult thoughts, memories, and emotions, but it will also help establish a practice for moving through the pain and returning back to yourself. Facing your trauma is not going to be easy—that's why it feels so tempting to just avoid the memories and try to forget. But avoidance only allows the grip of trauma to grab on tighter and not let go.

As you begin to work through the material in this book, you may experience strong negative emotions or even painful flashbacks of whatever it is that you've experienced. This may be a signal that you need to take a short break and return to the exercises when you feel ready. If you start to feel overwhelmed by memories or emotions, close the book and take a deep breath. Perhaps you need to take a walk or talk to someone you trust before returning to the material. Take as much time as you need before you begin again. Trust yourself to tackle the work at a pace that is best for you.

There's a lot of variability in how people respond to traumatic events. While one person may primarily suffer problems with negative thoughts about themselves or the world, someone else might be paralyzed by an overwhelming feeling of sadness or loss. A third individual may feel intensely disturbed by the way they've been acting since the event, such as neglecting their health or putting themselves in high-risk situations. Use your particular symptoms to help guide the order in which you approach the chapters.

If you are just beginning to understand your symptoms or want to determine what aspects of your experiences are related to the trauma you endured, begin with chapter 1, Understanding Trauma. If you are most troubled by feelings of fear, anger, or sadness, turn to chapter 2, which is all about your emotions. If your thoughts seem to be causing you the most trouble—for example, constantly blaming yourself for what happened or focusing on how cruel and unfair the world is—look at chapter 3, which focuses on your thoughts. Chapter 4 focuses on your body and provides guidance around the physical symptoms you may be experiencing and how to reconnect to your body in a healthy way. Finally, if your main concern is feeling isolated or you've been having problems in your relationships since the traumatic event, you may want to begin with chapter 5.

Also, keep in mind that your symptoms and thought patterns will shift over time. You may find yourself needing to revisit a section of the book that did not feel relevant before. Or you may encounter something or someone that triggers a memory, and all of a sudden you start having nightmares for the first time. This workbook is intended to help you with whatever you're facing on your road to healing—there is no right or wrong way to use it, nor is there some expected timeline for you to "get better."

Finally, it is worth noting that this workbook can be used on your own or alongside the assistance of a mental health professional. However, if you ever experience suicidal thoughts, strong urges to harm others, or frequent dissociation, or if you generally feel that you cannot function due to the level of trauma-related symptoms you are experiencing, please seek consultation with a mental health professional or call the National Suicide Prevention Lifeline at 1-800-273-8255 or 911 in the case of any emergencies.

CHAPTER 1

Understanding Trauma

What You'll Learn in This Chapter

In this chapter we will begin to explore what trauma is and the effect that it can have on your life. The chapter will include a discussion of the common symptoms that are associated with trauma and encourage you to begin reflecting on the range of symptoms you have experienced. You'll also be guided to begin writing the story of your trauma as a method of healing, as well as to start considering what changes you want to make and why.

What Is Trauma?

There are many ways to understand trauma. *Trauma* is an emotional response to a disturbing or distressing event or series of events. Unfortunately, traumatic experiences are pervasive in Western culture and can occur at any point in the human life span. National surveys have estimated that more than half of the adult population in the United States has experienced at least one major traumatic event. These experiences range from early childhood abuse to being robbed at gunpoint to experiencing a natural disaster. Trauma symptoms range from nightmares and flashbacks to a general sense of depression, anxiety, or unease.

Because traumatic experiences are vastly underreported, the true impact of trauma is likely even far more devastating and widespread than we know. Shame and self-blame are so common in the aftermath of trauma that many people never tell anyone the full story of what they experienced. For instance, a man who was sexually molested by his stepfather when he was 10 years old may have been so confused and disturbed by the experience that he spends his whole life trying to forget what happened and never tells another soul. A wife who is beaten by her husband each night but does not leave him will often begin to believe that she deserves the mistreatment. A combat soldier who witnesses children being slaughtered but is given a Medal of Honor for a successful mission may rightly decide that no civilian could understand the complexities of war. If a college freshman tells someone she was raped and is met with disbelief or questions about what she was wearing or whether she had too much to drink, she may learn it is easier to keep quiet. A middle-aged woman may have vague childhood memories of being scared and uncomfortable around her grandfather, but because he was a respected citizen and family member, she is left feeling unsure if something bad really happened or if there is simply something wrong with her.

If you're reading this book, you have likely been through something very painful. It's important to understand that trauma thrives on secrecy and self-doubt. If you can find a way to confront your darkest experiences, and if you can begin to give voice to these difficult things, you can start to heal. It might be scary to think about at first, but remember this: You are not alone.

EXERCISE: TRAUMATIC EXPERIENCES CHECKLIST

Instructions: The following list outlines common traumatic experiences. Generally speaking, the more incidents of trauma you have endured, the more trauma-related symptoms you will experience.

Put a checkmark beside every item that applies to you.

☐ When you were a child, did a parent or another adult hurt or punish you in a way that left a bruise, cut, or scratches or made you bleed?

☐ When you were a child, did someone five or more years older than you ever do something sexual with or to you?

☐ Have you been involved in a serious fire, earthquake, flood or other natural disaster?

☐ Have you ever been involved in a serious car accident?

☐ Have you ever been slapped, hit, beaten, or hurt in another way by someone you were in a romantic relationship with?

☐ Have you ever been physically attacked, assaulted, stabbed, or shot?

☐ Have you ever been hit, beaten, assaulted, or shot by the police or another government official?

☐ Have you ever been in the hospital because you were very sick or hurt and thought you may die?

☐ Have you ever witnessed someone get killed, badly hurt, shot, or assaulted?

PTSD: Basic Definition

Posttraumatic stress disorder (PTSD) is the clinical diagnosis most commonly associated with trauma. The hallmark symptoms of PTSD include nightmares, flashbacks, avoidance of trauma-related material, and intense emotional and/or physiological responses to internal or external reminders of the trauma—responses such as crying, sweating, or increased heart rate. Sometimes these symptoms will last for only a short period of time immediately following the trauma, but for many people the symptoms will persist chronically. Other common symptoms associated with trauma include depression, anxiety, irritability, difficulty falling or staying asleep, and physical symptoms such as digestive problems, difficulty concentrating, and problems with drugs and alcohol.

As a trauma survivor you may also experience problems in your relationships and dramatic shifts in your beliefs and how you view yourself. You may find it difficult to trust anyone—or become overly trusting of others and even put yourself in unsafe situations in order to regain a sense of connection to people. You may also find yourself treating others poorly as a means to feel less powerless. It is not uncommon for someone with deeply held religious beliefs to begin to question their relationship with God. Similarly, someone who once believed that good things happen to good people may come to view the world as cruel and unforgiving.

You may start to think of yourself as ineffective or permanently damaged when you once felt capable and strong. The effects of trauma can permeate all aspects of life. It may be immediately obvious that what you're experiencing is a result of the trauma you suffered, or there may be a lag of many years before you make the connection between a problem and the traumatic experience you endured. Each survivor's experience will be different. Try not to judge yourself for what you are experiencing, but rather approach yourself as you would a loved one, with gentle curiosity and understanding.

Long-Term Implications

Because of the widespread impact of trauma on our bodies, our mental health, and our brains, even a seemingly mild traumatic event can impact someone over an entire lifetime. If you had an immediate reaction to the trauma you experienced, such as panic attacks or nightmares in the days and weeks following the event, it was probably pretty clear to you what caused those things. However, when you don't seem to have an immediate reaction, or when your symptoms resolve relatively quickly after a trauma, it's easy to assume that the trauma didn't impact you or no longer impacts you—that you're "over it." Unfortunately, this is rarely the case.

The long-term effects of trauma can take longer to develop and are harder to recognize. For example, you may start to feel fewer emotions and develop a sense of "numbness," which can be your body's way of protecting you from emotional pain. You may have developed a general sense of mistrust toward others and over time notice that you have fewer interactions with others or fewer close friends. Your self-esteem may begin to erode, but you may falsely connect this feeling of incompetence to your abilities rather than to your trauma.

After a traumatic event, your brain will often go on "high alert" and will begin to notice possible threats in places you did not notice them before. As a result, you could experience more physical stress and/or muscle tension, which can lead to issues with chronic pain or stomachaches. The more you can identify your trauma reactions and actively engage in strategies for healing, the less likely it is the effects of your trauma will continue to haunt you in the long run.

Understanding Your Range of Symptoms

Although PTSD is the clinical syndrome most commonly associated with trauma, only a minority of trauma survivors actually develop PTSD. Other people will experience some of the symptoms associated with PTSD, such as nightmares or flashbacks, but may not develop the full syndrome. Others may experience depression, anxiety, substance abuse, or an eating disorder. Even the same symptom can be experienced differently by different people. For example, for one person a panic attack may manifest as an obvious panting and shortness of breath, while another person may experience it as blurred vision and chest pain.

The range of trauma reactions is widespread and complex. Symptoms also can change over time. While you may have been able to work through the intense and frequent nightmares you experienced immediately following your trauma, you may later develop a subtle but persistent feeling of sadness or difficulty experiencing pleasure doing the things that once brought you joy. The more you can understand what you are experiencing and why, the less difficult it will be to navigate your symptoms.

Anxiety

Anxiety can come in many forms, from general worry or apprehension about a range of events or activities, such as paying the bills or work performance, to marked fear about a certain situation, such as public speaking or being in enclosed spaces. It can take the form of a nearly constant stream of worried thoughts—*I'm running late again; I'm going to lose this client. What if I can't make rent this month? Why hasn't so-and-so called me back yet?*—to an abrupt surge of intense fear with accompanying physical sensations, like sweating or a racing heart. Extreme expressions of anxiety can take the form of hair pulling to the point of hair loss and/or skin picking that results in lesions.

Everyone worries. But when worry becomes excessive or overly focused on events that are either unlikely to happen or impossible to control, worry becomes problematic *anxiety*. Unlike worry, anxiety is often accompanied by a physical reaction. This can take the form of an overall sense of physical tension or more extreme physical reactions like sweating, increased heart rate, and difficulty breathing.

EXERCISE: ANXIETY CHECKLIST

Instructions: Select any of the following forms of anxiety that you experience. Although there is some overlap, the symptoms are roughly separated by the type of anxiety disorder they are associated with, in order to help you begin to identify the types of anxiety you are experiencing.

GENERALIZED ANXIETY

☐ Excessive anxiety or worry about many different events or activities

☐ Difficulty controlling your worry

☐ Anxiety or worry accompanied by feeling restless or on edge

☐ Anxiety or worry accompanied by having difficulty concentrating

☐ Anxiety or worry accompanied by irritability

☐ Anxiety or worry accompanied by muscle tension

☐ Anxiety or worry that disturbs your sleep

PANIC

☐ Experiencing abrupt surges of fear or discomfort that reaches a peak within minutes

If you selected the above symptom, what is this abrupt surge of fear accompanied by?

☐ Heart pounding

☐ Sweating

☐ Trembling or shaking

☐ Shortness of breath

☐ Feelings of choking

☐ Chest pain or discomfort

☐ Nausea

☐ Feeling dizzy or light-headed

☐ Chills or heat sensations

☐ Numbness or tingling sensations

☐ Fear of losing control

☐ Fear that you're dying

Exercise continues to next page

SEPARATION ANXIETY

☐ Excessive fear or anxiety concerning separation from an individual you are attached to

☐ Experiencing distress when you are separated from this individual or anticipate being separated from them

☐ Reluctance or refusal to go places because it will separate you from this individual

SOCIAL ANXIETY

☐ Fear or anxiety about social situations, especially when you anticipate being observed or scrutinized by others (such as eating in public, conversations with strangers, or public speaking)

☐ Fear that you will act in a way that will make your anxiety obvious

☐ Fear you will be embarrassed

☐ Avoiding or enduring social situations with intense fear or anxiety

SPECIFIC PHOBIA

☐ Fear or anxiety about a specific object or situation (e.g., blood or heights)

☐ Fear or anxiety is almost always immediately provoked by the object or situation

☐ The object or situation is actively avoided or endured with intense fear or anxiety

AGORAPHOBIA

☐ Fear or anxiety about using public transportation

☐ Fear or anxiety about being in open spaces (e.g., park or parking lot)

☐ Fear or anxiety about being in enclosed spaces (e.g., restaurant or movie theatre)

☐ Fear or anxiety about standing in line or being in a crowd

☐ Fear or anxiety about being outside of the home alone

Depression

Because depression is so common, most people are generally familiar with the term. However, there are a lot of cultural misconceptions about how depression affects us and what a depressed person needs. Depression is a physiological and psychological mental health condition that can manifest in multiple ways—it's not the same thing as "sadness," which is an *emotion*. This distinction is often blurred by the way we talk about depression in daily conversation. For instance, people often say they are depressed *about something* such as not getting a job, not having enough money, or not getting called back after a date when what they really mean is that they feel disappointed or sad. Depression is also much more persistent than sadness (i.e., you experience a depressed mood for most of the day for most days), and it is typically accompanied by a loss of interest or pleasure in things you used to enjoy and/or an overall feeling of numbness.

More severe forms of depression often include significant weight loss (without dieting), insomnia or hypersomnia (sleeping too much), feeling physically agitated or slowed down, feeling worthless or experiencing excessive guilt, and experiencing recurrent thoughts of death or thoughts of suicide.

There are two major types of depressive disorders: major depressive disorder and persistent depressive disorder (dysthymia). Major depressive disorder is typically more intense and severe but can be more short-term (e.g., two to three weeks), whereas persistent depressive disorder is typically less severe but more chronic (depressed mood for most days for at least two years). Anyone who experiences the more severe depressive symptoms (i.e., weight loss or suicidal thoughts) likely falls in the category of major depressive disorder. Of course, you can also experience a depressed mood or other symptoms of depression, especially in the aftermath of a traumatic event, without necessarily meeting criteria for a depressive disorder.

Instructions: Over the last two weeks, how often have you been bothered by any of the following problems?

Not at all (0) / Several days (1) / More than half the days (2) / Nearly every day (3)

Little interest or pleasure in doing things	
Feeling down, depressed, or hopeless	
Trouble falling or staying asleep, or sleeping too much	
Feeling tired or having little energy	
Poor appetite or overeating	
Feeling bad about yourself or that you are a failure or have let yourself or your family down	
Trouble concentrating on things, such as reading the newspaper or watching television	
Moving or speaking so slowly that other people could have noticed. Or the opposite—being so fidgety or restless that you have been moving around a lot more than usual	
Thoughts that you would be better off dead or of hurting yourself	

Depression Severity Total Score:

- 1–4   *Minimal depression*
- 5–9   *Mild depression*
- 10–14   *Moderate depression*
- *15–19   *Moderately severe depression*
- *20–27   *Severe depression*

*Please seek professional assistance if your depression severity reaches this level and/ or if you endorsed the last item on the above questionnaire and are experiencing suicidal thoughts.

Suicidal Thoughts

Suicidal thoughts are the most concerning symptom of depression (and other mental health disorders). **They are a sign that it's time to reach out to someone and seek help.** These thoughts may begin passively, such as thinking, *I would be better off dead* and may progress to wishing you were dead or imagining your funeral or your loved ones' reactions to your death. The most dangerous form of suicidal thinking is deciding how you would kill yourself and developing a suicide plan. Remember that these thoughts are likely a by-product of treatable mental health difficulties and that suicidal thoughts are still just thoughts, and thoughts can come and go. Most people who attempt suicide immediately realize that they do not want to die and go on to live fulfilling lives.

If you are experiencing any of these thoughts or symptoms, it's urgent that you seek professional mental health assistance. If it is easier, begin by calling a loved one; tell them about the thoughts you are having and ask them to help you seek help. Either way, it is important that you reach out to someone immediately. The National Suicide Prevention Lifeline (**1-800-273-8255**) is a free and confidential support line that is available 24 hours a day, seven days a week. The National Suicide Prevention Lifeline website (*SuicidePreventionLifeline.org*) contains other resources that may be helpful to you, including resources for finding a therapist or support group and tools to help you build a support network or develop a safety plan.

Flashbacks and Nightmares

In the immediate aftermath of a traumatic event, flashbacks and nightmares are among the most common symptoms you can experience, and they may continue long after the trauma occurred—especially if you continue to feel unsafe in your current environment.

Flashbacks can occur in any one of your five senses. For example, you may have visions of the trauma flash through your mind or "see" things in your mind that have happened to you. You may hear the voice of the person who hurt you or the sound of a gunshot. When a flashback involves multiple senses—for example, hearing *and* sight—you may literally feel like the trauma is happening to you in the moment, like you're reliving the horrible experience again. A flashback can last for a split second or stretch across minutes. Flashbacks may seem random at first, but remember that they can be triggered by any one of your senses. As you begin to observe the patterns of your flashbacks, you can start to notice the sights, sounds, smells, people, or situations that most often trigger them.

Trauma-related nightmares can be similar to flashbacks in that it feels like you are reliving the trauma you endured. But often, the content of the nightmare may only indirectly associate with the trauma. For example, someone who was raped may experience nightmares about being chased, held at gunpoint, or being attacked by animals. These nightmares can also be recurring or have reoccurring themes.

Following a flashback or trauma-related nightmare, you will likely experience intense physical and emotional reactions. The emotions you experience may be similar to those you experienced at the time of the original event, such as fear, horror, or helplessness. Similarly, the physical reaction you experience may include sweating, trembling, heart palpitations, and even feelings of choking or difficulty breathing.

EXERCISE: PTSD SELF-ASSESSMENT

Instructions: Review the symptoms below and circle *any* that affect you, regardless of how often or severely you experience it.

INTRUSIVE SYMPTOMS	AVOIDANCE SYMPTOMS	NEGATIVE THOUGHTS AND MOODS	ALTERATIONS IN PHYSIOLOGICAL AROUSAL AND REACTIVITY
Intrusive memories	Avoiding memories, thoughts, or feelings associated with the trauma	Trouble remembering parts of the trauma	Irritable behavior, angry outbursts, or acting aggressively
Nightmares	Avoiding external reminders of the trauma, such as people, places, and things	Having strong negative beliefs about yourself, other people, or the world	Taking risks or engaging in behavior that could cause you harm
Flashbacks		Blaming yourself or someone else for what happened	Constantly being on guard
Extreme emotional distress when reminded of trauma		Having strong negative feelings, like fear, anger, guilt, or shame	Feeling jumpy or easily startled
Strong physical reactions when reminded of trauma (e.g., heart pounding, sweating, or trouble breathing)		Loss of interest in activities you used to enjoy Feeling distant or cut off from people Having difficulty experiencing positive emotions	Having difficulty concentrating Having trouble falling or staying asleep

Next steps: Once you have identified the PTSD symptoms that you are experiencing, you can use this information to help you set goals and track your progress. Use the categories above to help you strategize your healing efforts.

For *intrusive symptoms*, you typically want to focus on processing what happened to you by spending time recalling, writing about, sharing, and analyzing your experiences. When you experience strong physical or emotional reactions to trauma symptoms, take a deep breath and remind yourself that you are safe. For *avoidance symptoms*, you want to slowly and safely confront the memories or places you have been avoiding (the best ways to do this will be discussed throughout the workbook). For *negative thoughts and moods,* focus on the strategies from chapters 2 (Your Emotions) and 3 (Your Thoughts). Finally, for *alterations in physiological arousal and reactivity,* turn to the exercise in chapter 4 (Your Body).

Dissociation

Dissociation is the feeling of being separated or disconnected from yourself or what you're experiencing. It's typically an internal experience and can be difficult to describe. Dissociative experiences fall on a continuum of severity from mild to potentially dangerous, the most common one being something we all recognize as "spacing out"—a momentary feeling of disengagement in which you lose track of what you were doing or the conversation you were having. If this cognitive-emotional disengagement becomes more frequent or extreme, people may start to say things like, "You seem a million miles away." Other dissociative experiences include feeling like you are outside of your body or standing outside yourself, watching things happen to you but not really being "there." Similarly, you may start to feel like you're living in a dream or movie or that the people around you are not real.

Amnesia and missing time are moderately severe dissociation symptoms. They are concerning, although not necessarily dangerous. Amnesia is the inability to remember important things in your life. Missing time is the experience of "zoning out" for what *you* think is moments, when in reality a much longer amount of time has passed. If you begin missing time during activities that demand your attention, like driving, it can become dangerous and may be a sign that you should seek help. Amnesia around certain aspects of your trauma experience—like the inability to remember a terrible car wreck—is very common. This is because when a traumatic experience is too overwhelming for your mind and body, dissociation of the senses commonly occurs as a way of protecting you from the full pain of the experience. With time and therapy, the memory of your trauma may return more fully.

The most serious and dangerous forms of dissociation are fugue states or identity alteration. You have experienced a fugue state if you have found yourself somewhere with no memory of how you got there or have traveled a significant distance without realizing it. You may be experiencing identity alteration if you feel like there are different people inside you or if people tell you that you sometimes act like a different person or use a different name. If you experience *any* of these symptoms, even once, it is important that you seek professional help immediately or call 911 if you are in immediate danger.

The Sidran Institute (Sidran.org) and the International Society for the Study of Trauma and Dissociation (ISST-D.org) both include a wealth of information and resources related to trauma and dissociation. The Sidran Institute includes a list of many hotlines, and their website and has a help desk (accessible via phone or e-mail) for further individualized help and assistance. The International Society for the Study of Trauma and Dissociation also includes a therapist directory.

EXERCISE: DISSOCIATION SELF-ASSESSMENT

Instructions: Over the past month, how often have you experienced the following?

0 = Never, 1 = Sometimes, 2 = Often, 3 = Very Often

"Spacing out"	
Staring into space	
Being absentminded or forgetful	
Not paying much attention to what is around you because you are in your own world	
Not having emotions about something that would typically make you upset	
Feeling emotionally numb	
Feeling like you are watching yourself from outside your body	
Feeling like you are in a dream	
Feeling like somewhere familiar (like your home) is no longer familiar	
People tell you that you did or said something that you don't remember	
Suddenly realizing hours have gone by and not knowing what you have been doing	
Feeling like there are different people inside you taking charge of your mind	
Suddenly finding yourself somewhere and having no idea how you got there	
Total Score:	

Next steps: The dissociation symptoms above are roughly organized in order of severity. If you endorsed the **last three symptoms** listed, especially with frequent severity, it is important that you **seek professional medical attention right away.** Otherwise, to begin to resolve milder dissociative symptoms, focus on strategies intended to help you reconnect your mind and body, like yoga and the other exercises outlined in chapter 4 of this workbook.

Panic Attacks

Panic attacks are characterized by an abrupt surge of fear accompanied by an intense physical reaction and/or fears of dying or losing control. The physical symptoms that can be experienced during a panic attack include the following:

- Heart pounding
- Sweating
- Trembling or shaking
- Shortness of breath
- Feelings of choking
- Chest pain or discomfort
- Nausea
- Feeling dizzy or light-headed
- Chills or heat sensations
- Numbness or tingling sensations

Because the physical symptoms of panic attacks are so intense, it is not uncommon for individuals experiencing panic attacks to show up at the emergency room, mistakenly thinking they're having heart attacks. People who suffer from panic attacks can also begin to develop persistent worry or anxiety related to experiencing *future* panic attacks and may begin to avoid behaviors they think might trigger panic or its symptoms, such as strenuous exercise, driving, or unfamiliar situations. Unfortunately, avoidant behaviors typically serve only to exacerbate the problem. When you're constantly trying to manipulate your life in order to prevent a panic attack, your fear of future panic attacks can increase, as the panic reaction starts to feel even more unpredictable and uncontrollable.

Physical Symptoms

Trauma has such a profound effect on our bodies' stress reaction that it has been associated with a wide range of physical symptoms and illnesses, which we'll discuss in depth in chapter 4 (Your Body). Due to the increased muscle tension associated with trauma and anxiety, survivors are more likely to experience headaches, chronic fatigue, and chronic pain. Trauma survivors are also more likely to experience problems with their cardiovascular and respiratory systems. They are also at increased risk to develop gastrointestinal disorders and diabetes.

The increased probability that a trauma survivor will develop such physical symptoms and/or illnesses is about 1.5 to 3 times that of someone who has not experienced a trauma. Traumatic experiences are associated with the development of an overactive stress response, which compromises general immune functioning. For this reason, trauma survivors are also more likely to catch common viruses and illness, such as the cold or flu.

Your Story

After a traumatic experience, it's natural to want to forget what happened to you. Avoiding pain is a universal human instinct—when we see a burning building, our impulse is to run to safety, not move in closer. The pull of avoidance can become so strong that many trauma survivors begin to avoid *anything* that might remind them of what happened—people, places, situations, or conversations that might trigger memories of the traumatic event. This avoidance can even include internal thoughts or feelings that remind you of what happened.

Avoidance behaviors may feel like they're working in the moment, but as the list of things you need to avoid continues to expand, your world starts to shrink, and your fear continues to grow. And despite everything you do to try to evade your trauma, the body and mind continue to process what happened *without you*. In the absence of your deliberate reflection or engagement, flashbacks, nightmares, and intrusive thoughts are your body's way of trying to work through and process what happened. In contrast, when you gently begin to confront what happened to you, you grow stronger, and your fear starts to wane.

In the absence of an actual threat or danger, intense emotions (like fear or sadness) are like waves. They reach a peak and eventually subside. One of the most effective ways to "ride" these waves and confront your fear in a safe environment is to write out the full story of what happened to you. Some survivors worry that if they put too much emphasis on their trauma experience, they allow it to become who they are; they don't want their whole identity to be defined as "rape survivor" or "childhood abuse survivor." That is completely understandable. But the only way to move *past* these painful experiences is to move *through* them. This requires you to deliberately reflect upon what happened to you and integrate that into your overall life story and self-concept. This important step in the healing process will help clear the way for you to grow into the person you want to become.

The process of writing your story can unfold quickly or over many weeks or months—whatever pace feels comfortable and safe to you. You may have a very clear memory and understanding of what happened, but it's also possible that you have significant memory gaps or struggle with questions about whether your experience qualified as a traumatic event. At this stage, the details of what you write are less important than simply starting the process.

When you are ready to begin, take out a blank sheet of paper, notebook, or journal. It's best to write in a quiet, safe space, at a time when you feel relatively calm (although as you begin the exercise, it's not uncommon to feel some physical discomfort or difficult emotions). Begin to write whatever comes to mind, and continue writing for as long as you can, or until you feel done. (Remember, "done" can just mean "done for now"—this is an ongoing process.) Later in the workbook, you'll find writing exercises that have more directive prompts or questions, but for now just write freely about what happened to you.

You may find that some aspects of your memory are particularly vivid. Take all the time you need to describe everything you remember, in as much detail as possible. Memories that trigger a particularly strong emotional or physical reaction can be underlined or otherwise highlighted in some way. When you draw a blank, simply note it with a question mark, and continue writing what you *do* remember. If the experience becomes too intense, take a deep breath and set it aside. Take a break if you need to, but be sure to return when you are ready. Over time, continue to write and rewrite your story until the narrative becomes more coherent.

EXERCISE: UNCOVERING EARLY CHILDHOOD TRAUMAS

Difficult early childhood experiences increase our risk of future health and mental health difficulties, and even our risk of experiencing certain types of trauma, like intimate partner violence. Taking a look at your history can reveal things about your present symptoms and challenges.

Instructions: Below is a list of difficult early childhood experiences that research has shown have a significant impact on our future health. Select any that apply to you, in order to begin to further understand the events or factors that may have contributed to the difficulties you are facing today.

- ☐ Childhood physical abuse
- ☐ Childhood sexual abuse
- ☐ Childhood emotional abuse
- ☐ Experiencing physical neglect as a child (such as not receiving adequate or stable food, clothing, and shelter)
- ☐ Experiencing emotional neglect as a child (such as having an absent or emotionally distant caretaker)
- ☐ Living in a household with domestic violence (regardless of whether or not violence was experienced directly)

- ☐ Witnessing or knowing that your mother (or maternal caretaker) was treated violently
- ☐ Substance abuse within the household
- ☐ Having a parent or caretaker with a mental illness
- ☐ Parental separation or divorce
- ☐ Growing up with an incarcerated household member

Instructions: Take a moment to reflect upon the areas in your life where trauma is affecting you. Begin with rating how much your trauma is present in each of the domains below. Once you have identified the impacted domains, take a moment to elaborate on *how* your trauma is showing up in this area.

1	2	3	4	5	6	7	8	9	10
Not at all		A little bit		Moderately		A lot		Extremely	

HOW MUCH IS YOUR TRAUMA SHOWING UP IN THIS AREA?

6	7	10
Emotions	Relationships	Thoughts

4	8	10
Beliefs	Daily Functioning	Health/Wellness

EXERCISE: ASSESSMENT ACROSS A RANGE OF SYMPTOMS

Instructions: Use the information below to determine which category (or categories) describes the symptoms you're experiencing. This information will further help you plan and prioritize your healing work.

	NO DIFFICULTY	SOME DIFFICULTY	SIGNIFICANT DIFFICULTY
Posttraumatic stress symptoms: Including flashbacks, intrusive thoughts and memories, avoidant behaviors, nightmares, difficulty concentrating, and hypervigilance or an increased startle response			X
Depression: Including a depressed mood and difficulty experiencing pleasure in activities you once enjoyed			X
Anxiety: Including generalized persistent worry, separation anxiety, and specific phobias			X
Panic: Experiencing an intense surge of fear, accompanied by physical sensations, either in response to a known trigger or seemingly at random		X	
Dissociation: Including feelings of being disconnected from your body, frequently spacing out or being absentminded, and/or periods of amnesia related to your trauma or generally		X	
Relationship difficulties: Including having difficulty trusting others or trusting too easily, having difficulty feeling close to others, or having difficulty sustaining stable relationships			X
Low self-esteem: Including feelings of incompetence, worthlessness, and excessive self-blame			X
Physical symptoms: Including frequent headaches, stomachaches, fatigue, chronic pain, or other illness			X
Risky behaviors: Including engaging in drug or alcohol misuse or other risky behaviors, such as speeding or engaging in promiscuous sex			X

Next steps: If all (or nearly all) of your symptoms fall under **PTSD**, **Depression**, **Anxiety**, or **Panic**, you may meet criteria for a diagnosis in this category. You would likely benefit from seeking additional consultation and support from a mental health professional. If you are experiencing symptoms in these areas, begin with the strategies outlined in chapter 2. For **dissociative symptoms**, start with the strategies in chapter 1. For **relationship difficulties** see chapter 5. For **low self-esteem** turn to chapter 3, and for **physical symptoms** begin with chapter 4. If you identify that you are engaging in **risky behaviors**, ideally seek treatment targeting the specific area of risk (such as substance abuse).

Trauma's Lingering Effects

Even after you have worked through most of your obvious trauma-related symptoms, trauma can still have lingering effects on your thoughts, feelings, beliefs, relationships, behavior, and health. For example, you may have developed a subtle belief that people can't be trusted or that if you trust someone you will get hurt. You may misperceive acts of caring as intrusive, sexual, or threatening in some other way. Many trauma survivors develop faulty beliefs around issues of power and control. Because the trauma experience is typically characterized by powerlessness and loss of control, you may begin to attempt to *overly* control certain aspects of your life—for example, never wanting your family to leave home without you. Conversely, you may generalize the feelings of powerlessness to other areas of your life and feel you have no ability to make positive changes or decisions in your life. You may stay in a job you hate because you feel a fundamental lack of agency. You may become generally more sensitive to situations that provoke strong emotions, such as difficult interactions with a loved one or attending a funeral, or conversely feel numb on such occasions. The more you can be aware of the ways that trauma has changed how you think, act, and feel, the more deliberate you can be in making decisions about how you want to live.

It's also important to note that the lingering effects of trauma are not all bad. There is a growing body of research about the posttraumatic growth that many survivors experience. Specifically, regardless of the level of distress they experienced, many survivors report finding a deeper sense of meaning in life and greater levels of overall life satisfaction. Some survivors report more easily recognizing what is truly important to them in life, increasing their acts of service to others, finding more meaningful relationships, and learning not to "sweat the small stuff."

This research suggests that such growth is associated with *deliberately* feeling, thinking about, and analyzing what happened to you—as opposed to passively engaging in a negative thought/memory loop in which the horrible experience plays on repeat in your mind. Posttraumatic growth is also associated with:

- Problem-focused coping
- Acceptance
- Positive reinterpretation

That's one reason why sticking with the exercises in this book—even when it's hard—is so important.

This Is Your Brain on Trauma

There are many neurological changes associated with trauma that can help explain the symptoms and sensations survivors experience. Some aspects of our brains, such as our threat detection processes, become overactive, which causes the brain to send distress signals to the body in circumstances where no real threat is present.

Other critical brain functions have a tendency to shut down or become less active. For example, under normal circumstances, the area of the brain known as the *thalamus*, which is involved in attention and concentration, acts as a filter to determine which sensory information is important for us to pay attention to. If we are driving and have noisy passengers in the car, the thalamus would help us ignore the sensory input of the passengers' chatter and allow us to keep our attention on the road. After a traumatic event, the thalamus becomes less active and may even shut down at times, leaving a trauma survivor's sensory floodgates wide open. As their brain becomes less effective at filtering out irrelevant sensory information, that same scenario—trying to drive with noisy passengers in the car—would become overwhelming and distracting, as would any random sights they might notice out of the corner of their eye.

In essence, trauma survivors start to live in a state of sensory overload. In response, the brain attempts to shut certain aspects of their experience down, which can then spill out into every area of the survivor's life.

Where Do You Stand?

Take a step back and look at your life as a whole. Where do you stand? What is going well, and what areas of your life do you want to see changes in? What connections do you see between the trauma you experienced and where you are in your life?

The trauma you endured was not your fault. It was something you could not control. This can easily foster a sense of helplessness or a tendency to give up in the face of challenges. Although you may not be the reason you ended up here, you are the only one who can make real changes in your life going forward. The following exercises are designed to help you begin to think about where you'd like to start.

This first exercise is designed to generate an overall vision of where you want to be in your life. As you do this, don't analyze how you're going to get there or conjure up all the obstacles you will need to overcome along the way. Just spend a few moments thinking about what you really want. Then, identify the first step toward getting there. This requires some faith in yourself. As Dr. Martin Luther King Jr. once said, "Faith is taking the first step, even when you don't see the whole staircase."

EXERCISE: IDENTIFY YOUR PRIORITIES

Instructions: Out of all the symptoms that you are experiencing, list the top five that are bothering you the most, and rate the severity of each symptom.

1	2	3	4	5	6	7	8	9	10
Not at all		A little bit		Moderately		A lot		Extremely	

SYMPTOMS BOTHERING YOU THE MOST

SYMPTOMS	SEVERITY RATING	FREQUENCY (# OF TIMES PER DAY, WEEK, OR MONTH)
1. Low - self esteem	10	everyday
2. Risky behaviors	10	5 x per week
3. physical symptoms.	10	everyday.
4. PTSD symptoms	10	everyday.
5. relationship difficulties	10	everyday/ relationship

(not in order).

These are your top priorities for *symptom reduction*. Keep in mind that you do not need to entirely eliminate a symptom to experience significant relief. This is why it's important to track the symptom frequency over time—to provide an objective measure of whether or not something is improving. The following chapters will provide you with concrete exercises and strategies to begin to work on reducing these symptoms.

EXERCISE: CHANGING YOUR BEHAVIOR

BEHAVIORS TO DECREASE

Instructions: List three behaviors you are engaging in that you know are not healthy and/or are likely making your symptoms worse (e.g., drinking too much or using drugs, spending time with people who make you feel unsafe, avoiding places or things you used to enjoy because they remind you of your traumatic experience), and note how frequently you are engaging in the behavior.

BEHAVIORS	FREQUENCY (# OF TIMES PER DAY, WEEK, OR MONTH)
1. using/finding a man	everyday.
2. Things i used to enjoy because they remind me of Trauma	everyday
3. eating unhealthy	everyday.

Instructions: Next, set a concrete goal for reducing one of the above behaviors:

GOAL: REDUCE	FREQUENCY (# OF TIMES PER DAY, WEEK, OR MONTH)
Reduce trying to find a man.	every other day (starting slow)

BEHAVIORS TO INCREASE

Instructions: Now, list three behaviors that you would like to increase (e.g., exercising, meditating, socializing, or going to a support group), and set a goal for how frequently you hope to engage in these behaviors. Remember to start small—set a goal that feels easy to meet. You can always build on this over time.

BEHAVIORS	FREQUENCY (# OF TIMES PER DAY, WEEK, OR MONTH)
1. excersizing	everyday.
2. Socializing	every week once.
3. finding new hobbies	every month.

Chapter Takeaways

- In this chapter, we learned what trauma is and how it can impact you. Because the impact of trauma is so complex and widespread, no two survivors will experience the exact same symptoms in the exact same ways.
- We reviewed the common symptoms associated with trauma and provided a framework for you to identify the symptoms you are experiencing. The range of symptoms we covered includes:

  - *Flashbacks and nightmares*
  - *Anxiety*
  - *Depression*
  - *Dissociation*
  - *Panic attacks*
  - *Physical symptoms*

- You were also encouraged to begin to write about your trauma and to identify your priorities for symptom reduction and behavior change.

CHAPTER 2

Your Emotions

What You'll Learn in This Chapter

In this chapter, we will explore the emotions that are common in the aftermath of a traumatic event, including fear, anger, and sadness. You will also begin to identify your personal triggers—internal or external feelings or events that set off intense emotions or memories—in order to help you feel more prepared to manage these painful experiences. You'll learn how you can work to change or shift your difficult emotions while at the same time learning to accept them as an integral piece of the human experience. We'll discuss how you can live a rich and full life, even if you continue to experience some trauma-related symptoms and memories. Finally, you will work on clarifying what's most important to you and begin to develop a plan for how you can live in a way that honors your values.

What Are You Afraid Of?

Not surprisingly, survivors often experience a great deal of fear and anxiety after a traumatic event. This is only natural after living through something painful, terrifying, and potentially life-threatening. Sometimes, the things you fear may seem logical and obvious, but other times your fear and anxiety will be triggered unexpectedly, and it may take some time to figure out what happened and why. If someone was assaulted in a park late at night, it would seem likely that particular parks, or even parks in general, would become a source of fear. It may also make sense that being out alone at night would trigger a panic reaction, as the circumstances would be similar to those during the assault. However, it may be less obvious to this person why silence or a particular style of jacket triggers a fear response. They may feel paralyzed by fear when faced with the prospect of going on a blind date or fall into a complete state of panic when approached by a stranger asking for directions.

The objects of your fear can be external, like crowded places, loud noises, or certain types of people. Or they can be internal—upsetting thoughts, emotions, or memories. You may develop anxiety related to internal cues, like certain feelings or physiological sensations such as an elevated heart rate or being short of breath. Some people may just generally feel a sense of constant anxiety, unease, or being "on guard," in essence anticipating a threat anywhere or at any time. Again, this makes sense, especially if the trauma you experienced was entirely unexpected or caught you off guard.

These intense feelings of fear and anxiety can have a profound impact on your behaviors and the way you react to situations. For example, I worked with a client named Kofi who was tortured by government officials in his home country in Africa. After safely resettling in America, he continued to experience intense fear anytime he saw someone in an official uniform, like a police officer. At these moments he returned to a total state of fight-or-flight and reported that his mind would go blank and he would experience pure terror and panic. As a result, when he saw police officers he would do anything he could to reduce his panic reaction, which often included abruptly running and/or driving in the opposite direction. As you can imagine, this response to *external* triggers increased Kofi's interactions with police officers, as his avoidance behaviors made him look suspicious.

Another client, whom I'll call Anna, was a competitive college track runner prior to being viciously date raped. After this traumatic experience, Anna experienced frequent panic attacks whenever she exercised. As she became short of breath from running, she was reminded of the physical sensations she experienced when trying to escape her attacker, which would in turn trigger distressing flashbacks and intrusive memories. In response to these *internal* physiological triggers, Anna had entirely stopped exercising and as a result had lost her track scholarship. All in an effort to avoid triggering this extreme panic reaction.

The more you're able to recognize what triggers your fear and anxiety, the less scary the subsequent feelings of panic or helplessness become, and the less you will feel caught off guard by your reactions. Additionally, once you identify your primary triggers, you'll be better able to proactively engage in strategies to counter your feelings of panic and helplessness, like taking a deep breath, reminding yourself that you're safe, or using mindfulness techniques to ground yourself in the present moment.

Instructions: Identify and describe any of the following potential triggers that cause you fear or anxiety.

PLACES:

Auburn, prisons, gig harbor, kent, Goodwill, Auburn House, Bus stops, des moines (all places I avoid).

SITUATIONS:

seeing Timothy, arguing, crying, being alone, some one upset.

PEOPLE:

mom, dad, anyone on mom & dad's side of the family.

Exercise continues to next page

OBJECTS:

Tobacco, Dolls, old family pictures of mom's Dad.

CONVERSATIONS:

rape, killing, burglaries

SOUNDS OR SMELLS:

yelling, drinking, alcohol, Ibuprofen, Tylonel, pills.

I love my mom but she is still a trigger.

EXERCISE: FEAR OF THE WORLD INSIDE

Instructions: Identify and describe any of the following potential triggers that cause you fear or anxiety.

THOUGHTS:

....

....

....

FEELINGS:

....

....

....

PHYSICAL SENSATIONS:

☐ Shortness of breath   ☐ Trembling

☐ Increased heart rate   ☐ Feeling dizzy

☐ Sweating

....

....

....

EXERCISE: WHAT ARE YOUR TRIGGERS?

Instructions: List your primary triggers.

If you are still having difficulty identifying your triggers, recall every little thing that was happening the last time you were triggered, and write it all down. This should give you some clues. You may need to do this a few times before you can start to pick out common patterns and themes.

Next, develop a preliminary plan for how to manage your fear reaction when it comes up. Because it is common to draw a blank or feel frozen in the midst of a panic reaction, it is best to pick simple, easy-to-remember strategies. For example, during the throes of a panic or fear response, you can take a deep breath, state out loud or to yourself that you were just triggered, or splash cold water on your face. Eventually you want to get to the point where the panic itself becomes its own kind of trigger—to prompt you to engage in these calming behaviors. Following a trigger reaction, you may want to call a loved one, journal, or listen to a favorite strong.

MY TRIGGERS:

1.

2.

3.

4.

5.

WHAT I CAN DO TO CALM DOWN WHEN I HAVE BEEN TRIGGERED:

1.

2.

3.

WHAT HELPS ME CALM DOWN FURTHER FOLLOWING A TRIGGER REACTION:

1.

2.

3.

Coping with Flashbacks

There are certain things you can do when you experience a flashback to help manage the anxiety and other strong feelings it may cause:

1. Begin by simply reminding yourself that you are having a flashback. It may even be helpful to say this out loud: "I am having a flashback."

2. Take slow, deep breaths. If you place your hand on your stomach, you should see it move with the inhalations and exhalations. This will send a signal to your body and brain that everything is okay and will help reverse the fight-or-flight response.

3. Engage your mind:

   • Count backward from fifty.

   • List everything you can think of from a given category (e.g., list all the sitcoms you can think of, pop songs, basketball teams, etc.).

4. Use your five senses to return to the present moment:

   • Splash water on your face or hold an ice cube.

   • Smell a favorite candle or scent.

   • Listen to music.

   • Observe your surroundings. Literally list everything you see to further engage your mind in the present moment.

EXERCISE: PREVENTING FLASHBACKS

LEARN YOUR WARNING SIGNS:

Although it will sometimes feel like your flashbacks come out of the blue, there is often an early physical or emotional warning sign. This might include shortness of breath, sweating, a specific thought or type of thinking, or a change in your mood. Once you identify your own early warning signs, list them here:

_____

_____

_____

IDENTIFY YOUR TRIGGERS:

Experiences that trigger your flashbacks may be similar to the triggers you identified in the preceding exercises, or they may be slightly different. Again, if you are having difficulty identifying the experiences, thoughts, feelings, or sensations that trigger your flashbacks, notice what is happening the next time you have a flashback, or think back to the last time you had one and write down everything you can remember about what was happening or what you were thinking about right before.

_____

_____

_____

Continue to process what happened to you. The more you continue to work through and confront what happened to you, the more you will understand your trauma reactions and experience some relief from your trauma-related symptoms.

What Should You Do with Your Anger?

Anger is an incredibly common emotion in the aftermath of trauma. If you have been through a horrible, life-shattering event, it makes total sense. You may feel angry at the person or people who hurt you, angry that this thing happened to you, angry at everyone who didn't have to go through what you did, angry at the world or life in general, angry at yourself, angry at your family, angry at anyone trying to help you, angry at strangers. *Your anger is valid.* You have a right to feel it. The challenge becomes, what do you do with it? How can you use your anger as a way to learn and grow, as opposed to letting it become destructive?

Anger is not inherently bad or wrong—when it is used constructively. It can help you recognize that you're in pain and identify the areas where you need further healing. It can also help you be more honest with others. However, when used *de*structively, anger encourages you to act out against yourself or others. This can manifest in your unwillingness to do anything to make your life better or turn into feelings of lasting bitterness. One way to differentiate between constructive and destructive anger is to consider the level of intensity. Constructive anger usually feels moderately intense and can be used to understand something better and/or take positive action. Destructive anger is often highly intense and frequent and is typically acted out in dangerous or destructive ways.

EXERCISE: PHYSICALLY RELEASING YOUR ANGER

Unfortunately, you can't fight your way out of anger. There is a general cultural assumption that anger builds up inside us and then needs to be released (hence the term "letting off steam"). On the contrary, research has found that aggressive acts, like hitting a punching bag or pillow, may make us feel better in the short term but ultimately serve to increase our anger because of the anger-aggression association our brain makes with these activities.

However, there are some strategies you can use to physically release the energy of anger from your body, without encouraging feelings of aggression.

- Take a deep breath in. As you exhale, envision releasing the anger from your body. You may want to accompany your breath with the thoughts "breathing in calm" and "exhaling anger."
- Go to a private space and shake your body and limbs, again envisioning that you are releasing anger from your body.
- Exercise. Go for a run, take a yoga class, do jumping jacks, or engage in whatever your favorite form of exercise is.
- Put on your favorite song and have a private dance party.

EXERCISE: DEAR ANGER: SYMBOLICALLY RELEASING YOUR ANGER

Instructions: Use this exercise to write a letter to one of the main sources of your anger. This could be the person who hurt you, or it could be more generally addressed to the world or God. If you primarily direct your anger toward yourself, you can write yourself a letter. It can feel tempting to fill all the pages with hatred and curse words, but this tends to fuel destructive forms of anger. Instead, with as little bitterness as possible, honestly and clearly explain why you are angry and the hurt that you feel. If you can find it within yourself to forgive the source of your anger, do so. Or, if you're not quite ready for that, write about what you wish would happen going forward. This is one of the best ways to release anger. Remember that hurt people hurt people. Whoever caused you pain is also in pain.

Once you are done, some people find it helpful to symbolically release the letter. You can do this by ripping it up, burning it, or crumpling it into a ball.

Dear

What's Underneath Your Anger?

Anger is sometimes called a *secondary emotion* because we often turn to it in order to avoid other more vulnerable feelings like fear, hurt, helplessness, and sadness. In general, the most aggressive patients I have ever worked with in psychiatric facilities or other mental health settings had the most severe trauma history. In these extreme cases, the individuals learned that it was easier to consider everyone an enemy and to keep other people at a distance with hostility and physical aggression than to risk getting hurt again. Anger is always a signal that something is wrong and needs to be dealt with—e.g., an unmet need, a painful emotion, or an unresolved fear. The next time you feel a surge of anger, take some time to examine what other feelings may be there, lurking underneath it. The more vulnerable feelings of pain and fear also need to be expressed.

What Should You Do with Your Sadness?

Sadness is another common emotion that stems from experiencing a traumatic event. You may feel sadness about something you lost, whether that loss was a person, your innocence, the ability to feel carefree, or something else important to you. Or you may simply feel sadness or depression that's not associated with any one particular thing. Sadness and depression often co-occur but can also exist independently. You may feel a deep sadness while also continuing to feel joy, whereas depression can dull your ability to feel *anything* fully and often robs you of the ability to take pleasure in the things that once made you happy.

One client I worked with, Denise, lost her two young daughters in a tragic car accident. She would sob through entire sessions, barely managing to get a few words out. When she did talk, she described her sadness as feeling like a knife in her chest. She felt guilty doing anything that once brought her joy, wondering how she could ever be happy when she had lost her whole world. Denise eventually found some purpose by connecting with and helping other mothers who had also lost children.

For an adolescent client named Caitlin, her sadness and depression looked very different. After being raped twice on two separate occasions, she also barely talked, but not because she was crying. Instead she sat quietly, staring into the distance, looking listless and blank. She described feeling empty and having no interest in other people or the things she used to love. The only thing she still enjoyed was smoking pot; she described being high as the closest she ever came to feeling happy or feeling *something*. Caitlin slowly came alive again when she agreed to start trying to do some of the things she used to enjoy, like costume design and going to the beach.

According to the Dalai Lama, focusing too much on ourselves is one of the primary sources of negative emotions. We can begin to shift these negative emotions by focusing our attention on the needs of others. Psychological research has been consistent with this philosophy, having found that engaging in altruistic or compassionate acts toward others not only reduces our feelings of sadness and other negative emotions but increases feelings of joy and overall life satisfaction.

Another effective approach to changing any negative emotion—including sadness—is to act as if you were not experiencing the emotion in the first place. For instance, if you're feeling anxious about some upcoming interaction (with your mom, with your boss, with your significant other), you act as if you were feeling confident. The trick is to wholeheartedly embrace the actions and behaviors associated with that opposite feeling. When you are feeling deeply sad, think about what you would be doing if you were happy. For starters, you would probably be smiling. Or at the very least, your brow would be unfurrowed.

Because depression is often characterized by wanting to do nothing, one of the most powerful antidotes to feeling depressed is to simply do *something*. The clinical term for this phenomenon is *behavioral activation*, and it has been found to be one of the most effective treatment tools for combating depression. For many people who are battling depression, even simple activities can feel very difficult. That is why it can be helpful to intentionally schedule your daily activities in the same way you would schedule meetings for work. You may commit to going for a walk at 10 a.m. on one day and then commit to meeting a friend for coffee the following afternoon. It's best to start simple to avoid getting overwhelmed.

EXERCISE: WHEN YOUR SADNESS FEELS TOO DEEP

In general, you will experience more effective symptom reduction if you work toward being able to fully feel and accept your emotional experiences. But when your sadness (or any other difficult emotion) feels too strong to bear, you may need to engage in distraction techniques until the intensity of the emotion subsides.

- Distract your body:

    - *Splash cold water on your face or take a cold shower.*
    - *Engage in intense exercise (like running or jumping) to expend your physical energy.*
    - *Engage in deep diaphragmatic breathing, counting each breath. When your mind wanders, start back at one.*

- Distract yourself with a different emotion:

    - *Watch a brief comedy sketch.*
    - *Watch a brief video that invokes a positive emotion.*
    - *Watch a scary movie.*

- Distract yourself with activities:

    - *Organize a drawer in your house.*
    - *Go for a walk.*
    - *Call a friend.*

- Distract yourself with thoughts:

  - *Pick up a book or magazine and read the words out loud, backward.*
  - *Write out the lyrics to a favorite song.*
  - *Do a crossword puzzle or other mental challenge.*

- Distract yourself with kindness:

  - *Write someone a thoughtful card or e-mail.*
  - *Make a food or toiletry bag and distribute it to someone in need.*
  - *Do something thoughtful for a friend.*

Treatments for Trauma

Research has found that trauma-focused psycho-therapies are the most effective method of treatment for posttraumatic stress disorder (PTSD) and other trauma-related symptoms. Three of these therapies are briefly highlighted below.

Prolonged Exposure (PE) is a trauma treatment that was originally developed by Edna Foa, PhD. This approach primarily targets the avoidance symptoms that are characteristic of PTSD and trauma exposure by assisting the client in confronting the details of the trauma they experienced and the situations that continue to frighten them. This is done through *imaginal* and *in vivo* exposure techniques. Imaginal exposure involves confronting the memories of your trauma by recalling it in detail and retelling it to your therapist and even listening to audio recordings of yourself describing the experience. In vivo exposure involves confronting real-life situations that continue to frighten you, like getting on a crowded subway. You will also be taught breathing and relaxation techniques to help you through these exposure experiences and will be supported by your therapist along the way. With repeated exposure, the level of distress aroused by these difficult memories and situations should subside.

Cognitive Processing Therapy (CPT), which was developed by Drs. Patricia Resick, Candice Monson, and Kathleen Chard, targets the way you think about yourself and the world following a traumatic event. Many trauma survivors start to believe that they are to blame for what happened and/or that the world is a dangerous place. This type of thinking typically exacerbates trauma-related symptoms and can keep you from doing the things you used to enjoy. CPT helps you learn to examine your thinking and to determine if there is an alternative thought process that may be more accurate (or simply more helpful to you). CPT also encourages you to write in detail about your trauma experience in order to help you identify the thoughts and beliefs you hold about what happened. You will also focus on specific areas of your life that were likely impacted, including your sense of safety, trust, control, self-esteem, and intimacy.

Eye Movement Desensitization and Reprocessing (EMDR) was developed by Francine Shapiro, PhD. During EMDR you recall upsetting memories or details of the traumatic event while simultaneously paying attention to a back-and-forth movement, sensation, or sound. You then continue to recall the same memory until doing so no longer causes you physical or emotional distress. While it is clear that EMDR works, there is still some disagreement about *how* it works. Specifically the research is mixed as to whether or not the back-and-forth movement is a necessary part of the treatment or if simply processing the trauma memories is what helps reduce the symptoms.

Feeling Your Pain and Living Your Life

Suffering is part of the human condition. No matter how skilled we become at managing difficult emotions, we will continue to feel pain in our lives. It's actually a trap to believe we can avoid pain and uncomfortable feelings. When we actively try to avoid difficult emotions or push them aside, they paradoxically grow bigger and have more control over our lives.

Imagine someone with a fear of flying who is invited to a loved one's wedding across the country. Because they're so terrified of flying, they feel flooded with relief when a work-related excuse causes them to miss the wedding. But the next time a situation like this arises, will this person be more or less likely to get on the plane? Less—because the relief they felt (however short-lived) the last time will reinforce this avoidance behavior. This does nothing to reduce their fear, though. If anything, the fear will grow bigger as they continue to convince themselves that it is so powerful it should be avoided at all costs.

Now, consider the alternative. What if this person decided to get on the plane in spite of their fear? They will likely feel worried and anxious leading up to the flight and may even experience a distressing surge of anxiety on the plane. They may grip the seat handles the entire time, assume that each turbulent bump means the plane is about to crash, and find they're drenched in sweat when the plane lands. But they see the calm, matter-of-fact nature of their fellow passengers, too. And they land without incident.

Will this person continue to go out of their way to avoid flying? Maybe—but most likely they'll be less afraid to fly the next time something like this comes up. They will have shown themselves the experience of making it through a plane ride relatively unscathed, and as unpleasant a ride as it may have been, it was not as bad as they had built it up to be. Now their fear of flying will begin to shrink, even if only slightly, because deep down they know that they can make it through a flight. They have proof.

And guess what else? This person also gets to have a wonderful time with their friends and family instead of staring wistfully at photos of an event they missed out on.

The alterative to fighting your painful emotions is surprisingly simple: Just let them happen. Allow life to flow through you—the good, the bad, and the ugly. Research has shown that trauma survivors who start with equal levels of PTSD symptoms have dramatically better outcomes when they allow themselves to experience the difficult memories, thoughts, and feelings as opposed to consistently attempting to avoid them. The key to living a meaningful and balanced posttrauma life is to continue to live fully despite the symptoms and painful memories you may carry with you.

Your symptoms will wax and wane over time or even change form completely as you evolve and grow. You may experience nightmares and flashbacks at one point and depression at another. The pull of avoidance will always be there. But the more you can fully accept your experiences and emotions as they are, the less caught up you'll be in what is essentially a rigged game. Start to focus more on what you want in life and less on what you *don't* want. What would make your life more meaningful? How can you start to have those experiences?

EXERCISE: INVITING DISCOMFORT

This is an experiential exercise. You may want to read through the below text once in its entirety and then read it through a second time, pausing after a few lines to close your eyes and try to experience what the text is talking about. Don't force it. Let whatever comes up come up.

- Which emotion do you have the hardest time with? Is it loneliness? Sadness? Fear? Close your eyes and imagine inviting that emotion to come. Think of something that makes you feel that uncomfortable emotion. If it never shows up, that is okay, too. What is important is that you were willing to feel it.
- If the difficult emotion shows up for you, observe what you are feeling. See if you can sit with it. Work on accepting it fully. Accept it into your mind, heart, and body. If other difficult emotions arise, allow them to come as well. If painful or difficult thoughts come up, observe and accept them for what they are: merely thoughts.
- Accepting a difficult emotion does not mean that you approve of or accept the facts of painful thoughts or events. You are simply accepting the sensations of the feeling.

EXERCISE: VALUES WORKSHEET

Instructions: This exercise is intended to help you work through what is important to you and how much your day-to-day life reflects those values. Complete the Importance column in its entirety before moving to the Action column. This exercise is intended to be completed quickly in order to discourage you from overthinking. You may even find it helpful to set a five-minute timer.

VALUE	IMPORTANCE How important is each value to you? Rate on a scale of 1 to 10, with 1 meaning "not very important" and 10 meaning "very important/a deeply held value."	ACTION How much are your daily actions in line with your values? Rate on a scale of 1 to 10, with 1 meaning "I wish I were doing much more in this area" and 10 meaning "I'm living according to this value."
Family		
Friends		
Work		
Learning		
Fun/Recreation		
Spirituality		
Health/Fitness/Wellness		
Community		
The Environment		
Beauty/Aesthetics		

EXERCISE: MINDFULNESS OF EMOTIONS

Mindfulness and acceptance work hand in hand. If you are working toward learning to accept difficult emotions, it is also important to become aware of your full emotional experience. This worksheet will help you practice this.

The worksheet will be easier to complete and more relevant when you are in the midst of or have recently experienced a difficult emotion of at least moderate intensity. You may want to photocopy this worksheet prior to completing it, so you can practice this skill with a range of emotions.

What emotion are you experiencing?

What happened right before you experienced this emotion? In other words, what do you think brought this emotion on?

What thoughts or beliefs did you have about the situation that led to your emotion?

Exercise continues to next page

Did anything make you more vulnerable to experiencing this emotion (e.g., lack of sleep, being hungry, being intoxicated, already being in a bad mood, etc.)?

What is happening in your body? (E.g., are you tensing any muscles? What is your facial expression? Did your heart rate change? What is your posture?)

What did you feel like doing when you felt this emotion?

What did you actually do or say when you felt this emotion?

EXERCISE: WHERE DO I WANT TO START?

I want to make the following change or changes:

The reasons why I want to make these changes are:

I plan to start making these changes by taking the following steps:

The people in my life can help me make these changes by (ideally, take this a step further and ask these people for the help you need):

What could get in the way of making these changes?

Exercise continues to next page

How will I overcome these barriers?

....

....

I will know my plan is working when . . .

....

....

Chapter Takeaways

In this chapter we explored various emotions and how they may have been impacted by the trauma you experienced. My hope is that you've come away from this with:

- A better understanding of some of the core difficult emotions, including fear, anger, and sadness.
- An initial understanding of your personal triggers, both inside you and in the outside world.
- Strategies for changing and releasing difficult emotions when you need to.
- Skills to become more mindful and accepting of your emotional experiences.
- An understanding that pain and a full, joyful life are not mutually exclusive.
- A better understanding of what is important to you.
- An initial plan for how to start making changes toward a life that is full of the things that matter most to you.

CHAPTER 3

Your Thoughts

What You'll Learn in This Chapter

In this chapter we will examine our thoughts and how our thinking influences how we feel and act. Trauma often changes the way we think by changing or distorting our perceptions of things like safety, risk, trust, and control. To address this, we'll learn about and use exercises from Cognitive Processing Therapy (CPT), which has been found to be very effective in treating trauma by targeting thoughts and underlying beliefs.

You will learn about some common problematic thought patterns and how to identify the specific thoughts and beliefs that may be holding you back in your recovery. You'll be provided with tools to begin challenging any distorted or unhealthy thinking you may be engaging in and learn some ways to break the link between these thoughts and your behaviors.

Finally, you will begin to write a new story about your life and what happened to you. This new story and way of thinking will help you acknowledge what you've been through while hopefully allowing you to let go of some of the beliefs that are holding you back.

Trauma Changes How You Think

Trauma fundamentally changes the way you think about yourself and the world. You may start to believe that the world is a hostile place where you're always under attack. You may think that you're to blame for what happened and/or that you are helpless and have no control over what happens to you.

Most survivors also experience significant changes in their self-esteem or self-concept. After years of being in a domestically violent relationship in which she was repeatedly sexually violated, a trauma survivor named Maria described feeling like she was "nothing more than a body meant to be used and discarded." After living through a major natural disaster, another survivor named Sharon developed exaggerated fears of leaving her home anytime there was even a minor shift in the weather.

These forms of distorted thinking typically exacerbate trauma-related symptoms and can keep you from doing the things you used to enjoy, forming meaningful connections with others, and living a life in which you feel safe and content.

Because of the impact that trauma has on brain functioning, you may also experience racing thoughts, memory loss, difficulty concentrating, and problems forming new memories. These are all normal responses to trauma, and with some time and effort, you can begin to rebalance your brain by reactivating the logical, sequential parts of your brain and beginning to calm those parts that may have become overactive since the trauma.

What Is Cognitive Processing Therapy?

Cognitive Processing Therapy (CPT) is a therapeutic approach that targets changes in thinking that are typical following a traumatic event, including changes in the way you think about yourself and the world. The goal of CPT is to help you learn to examine your thinking and determine if there is an alternative point of view. Because of how profoundly trauma changes your thinking, a part of this work requires you to go back and revisit the traumatic event in order to understand how your current—often unhelpful—thought processes developed.

When we're exposed to information that doesn't match our view of the world, we typically do one of two things in response: We either change the information to fit our beliefs ("maybe I wasn't really raped") or we change our beliefs ("maybe bad things do happen to good people"). Sometimes, belief changes become extreme, such as thinking *I always make mistakes* or *only bad things happen to me* (which is sometimes called *overgeneralization*).

In CPT, the first step is to work on integrating the traumatic experience into your belief systems and memories so that you begin to come to terms with what happened. The next step is to modify any overgeneralized beliefs. Some of our emotions are biologically hardwired—like feeling fear in response to danger or sadness in response to loss—but many of our emotions, such as guilt and shame, are thought to be "manufactured" as a result of faulty thinking. The good news is manufactured emotions often dissipate following the changes in thinking CPT helps cultivate.

Cognitive tasks, including something as simple as labeling objects, activates the logical part of our brains, like the prefrontal cortex, which in turn helps regulate the emotional parts of the brain like the amygdala. Using your words to talk about and analyze the traumatic event calms overactive emotional responses.

The goal of CPT's therapeutic exercises, which we'll explore below, is to increase flexibility in your thinking and support your ability to think critically about what you've been saying to yourself about why the traumatic event happened and what it means about yourself, others, and the world around you.

"Stuck points" are negative trauma-related thoughts or beliefs that are exaggerated or distorted in some way that will ultimately impede your recovery. Specifically, stuck points are the problematic ways you evaluate the traumatic event, like the common belief that if you'd acted differently you could have kept it from happening. These beliefs could be new (posttrauma), or the trauma might have served as confirmation of some negative beliefs you already held. For instance, someone who, prior to a traumatic event, placed great trust in authority figures like the police may begin to develop a new belief that police are worthless and untrustworthy because they weren't able to respond quickly enough to prevent an assault. In contrast, someone who went through a similar scenario but already had difficulty trusting authority would confirm their long-standing beliefs following the trauma.

If you've been thinking the same things over and over again ever since your traumatic event, without reconsidering those thoughts or exploring alternative ideas, the thoughts have likely become habitual and entrenched in your beliefs. In order to begin to shift those thought patterns, you must approach your thoughts and beliefs with an open mind and a willingness to challenge your assumptions.

CPT was developed to treat a range of disorders and mental health difficulties, including PTSD, depression, anxiety, personality difficulties, problems with substance use, and difficulties surrounding self-esteem and self-concept. CPT has been heavily researched, and there is strong evidence for its effectiveness across a variety of populations. Study results indicate that participants have seen significant decreases in self-reported PTSD as well as in other trauma-related mental health difficulties, both during treatment and at six-month follow-ups.

Common Problematic Thought Patterns

Sometimes called *cognitive distortions* or "stinkin' thinkin,'" the following list of problematic thought patterns has been associated with both depression and PTSD. Learning about these patterns can help you begin to identify the thinking that may be causing you increased distress.

We all engage in distorted thinking at times, but when these thought patterns become habitual, significant emotional distress can result. Once you learn to identify the ways in which your thinking can be distorted, your goal becomes to "catch it and correct it" before the thoughts lead to negative emotions.

Magnification and Minimization: This occurs when you either exaggerate or minimize the importance of something. For example, you may discount your achievements but become excessively focused on your mistakes.

Catastrophizing: Focusing your attention on the worst possible outcome of a situation and assuming that it is a likely possibility.

Overgeneralization: When you make a broad interpretation from one event. For example, you might think, *I felt awkward on that date. I am always so awkward.* Or, *I got the wrong answer to that question. I am always so stupid.*

Magical Thinking: Linking actions to unrelated situations. For example, believing that bad things will not happen to you because you are a good person.

Personalization: This occurs when you take things too personally or relate situations to yourself that may actually have nothing to do with you. For example, *She looks pissed off. I must have done something wrong.*

Jumping to Conclusions: Making assumptions or interpreting the meaning of a situation with little or no evidence.

Mind Reading: When you interpret the thoughts and beliefs of others without adequate evidence. *He didn't invite me to go to lunch. He probably hates me.*

Fortune-Telling: When you assume that a situation will turn out badly without adequate evidence. *I will never stop feeling this way.*

Emotional Reasoning: Assuming that your emotions reflect reality. *I feel angry, therefore you must have treated me badly* or *I am sad, therefore I am not going to get what I want.*

Disqualifying the Positive: Focusing only on the negative aspects of a situation while ignoring the positive aspects. For example, you may receive many compliments from your friends but remember the single piece of negative feedback someone told you.

"Should" Statements: Fixating on beliefs that things should be a certain way. *I should be married by now. I should be happy.*

All-or-Nothing Thinking: Thinking in absolute terms, such as *always*, *never*, and *every*: *I never do anything right. I am always going to be lonely.*

EXERCISE: FINDING YOUR STUCK POINTS

Instructions: Identifying the stuck points in your thinking can be difficult, especially if the thought or belief is something you've been carrying around for a while. Some people know right away which of their thought patterns are problematic, while others may need time to figure it out. If you're not sure what your stuck points are after reviewing the tips below, make your best guess or simply pick a thought that makes you feel bad. If you don't notice a change in your emotions or behaviors after challenging and/or modifying the initial stuck point(s), try to find more stuck points or beliefs.

TIPS FOR IDENTIFYING YOUR STUCK POINTS

- Review the list of common problematic thought patterns on page 46. Stuck points often fall into one of those categories.
- Stuck points may be thoughts about your understanding of *why* the traumatic event happened or thoughts or beliefs about yourself, others, and the world that changed after the traumatic event.
- Stuck points may be if-then statements, such as "if I trust someone, I will get hurt."
- Stuck points often include extreme or exaggerated language, such as *always*, *never*, *every time*, *everything*, or *everyone*.
- Stuck points are not feelings, behaviors, facts, or questions.
- Examples of stuck points:
  - *Because I didn't tell anyone, I let the abuse happen.*
  - *I am worthless.*
  - *I am damaged.*
  - *No one can understand what happened to me.*
  - *If I am happy, I am not honoring his/her memory.*
  - *Other people should not be trusted.*
  - *If I get close to someone, I will get hurt.*
  - *If I fought harder, the abuse wouldn't have happened.*
  - *If I express my emotions, I will lose control.*
  - *If I think about what happened, I will never get it out of my mind.*
  - *I deserved what happened to me.*
  - *If I wasn't drinking, it never would have happened.*
  - *I let it happen.*
  - *I caused the abuse because I couldn't keep my mouth shut.*

Exercise continues to next page

● My stuck points:

1. ....

2. ....

3. ....

EXERCISE: CHALLENGING YOUR STUCK POINTS

Note: You may want to photocopy this worksheet, so you can repeat the process for multiple stuck points.

LIST ONE OF YOUR STUCK POINTS:

....

....

....

How much do you believe this point (from 0% to 100%)? ....

CHALLENGING QUESTIONS:

What is the evidence for this point?

....

....

....

What is the evidence against this point?

Does your stuck point include all the information available to you?

Is the point extreme or exaggerated in any way (does it include any extreme words that could be modified like always, never, should, *or* everyone*)?*

Is your stuck point based more on feelings than facts?

Exercise continues to next page

Is your stuck point helpful to you? Or making you feel better?

_____

_____

NEW ALTERNATE THOUGHT/BELIEF:

_____

_____

How much do you believe this new thought (from 0% to 100%)? _____

_____

_____

_____

I Think, Therefore I DO

As illustrated above, thoughts, emotions, and behaviors are interconnected and influence each other. Because of this, it can feel like your thoughts *cause* your behavior. If you feel a surge of anger and then lash out at someone, it can feel like you had no control over your response. Similarly, if you feel scared or hurt, you might feel like you have no choice but to retreat into solitude, pull the covers over your head, or have a drink to lessen the pain. But the truth is, feelings and thoughts don't *cause* behaviors. We have a lot of freedom to choose how we want to respond, even to the most painful memories or emotions, as long as we stay aware of how our thoughts and feelings influence our actions.

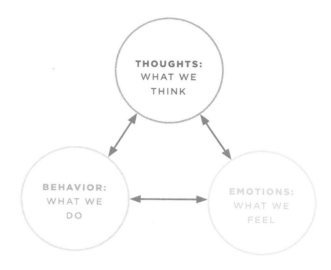

The first step in breaking the link between your thoughts and your behaviors is to become more aware of each of those things in the moment. When you feel like doing something in response to an emotion, try to identify the *thought* that preceded your urge to behave a certain way. Thoughts can become very automatic and even unconscious, but with practice you can learn to "catch" your thinking. Before you act, pause. Take a deep breath and consider the consequences of your actions and possible alternative ways to respond. Just taking a small pause can introduce a whole range of alternatives, many of which may be healthier or more productive than your first impulse.

The good news is, because thoughts, feelings, and interactions are all connected, if you make a change in one area, changes will follow in the others. As you change your thinking, your emotions and behaviors will also change. If someone says something offensive to you, you may automatically have the thought *I was disrespected*, feel angry, and verbally lash out at the person. In certain circumstances—if this person were your boss, for example— that could have terrible consequences. But if you take a moment to pause and consider alternative explanations for their behavior, such as "maybe she's having a bad day," or "maybe I misinterpreted what she was saying," you will likely react in a more thoughtful, less destructive way. Similarly, if you change what you *do*, it will impact your thoughts and feelings.

If you're feeling depressed and having negative thoughts, just going outside and standing in the sunshine for a while can often facilitate a shift in both your mood *and* your thought patterns. A simple shift can have tremendous benefits.

> Note: You may want to photocopy this exercise so that you can complete it for multiple different situations. There is ample room provided on the worksheet so that you can fully think through the automatic thought that comes up for you.

SITUATION

EMOTIONS

AUTOMATIC THOUGHT
(What is the first thought that comes to mind?)

BEHAVIOR URGE
(What do you *feel like doing*?)

ALTERNATIVE/BALANCED THOUGHT
(List some alternative explanations for your initial thought.)

ALTERNATIVE BEHAVIORS
(What are some other things you could do in this situation? Consider what behaviors would be most helpful to you in the long run.)

ALTERNATIVE BEHAVIORS
(What are some other things you could do in this situation? Consider what behaviors would be most helpful to you in the long run.)

WHAT I DID

Mindfulness Practices

Mindfulness practices are gaining increasing attention in the field of psychology and psychotherapy. Rooted in ancient techniques, mindfulness practices have been shown to reduce a wide range of psychological symptoms and disorders, including anxiety, depression, and substance abuse. Mindfulness is often confused with meditation, and although there is some overlap, mindfulness is more of an attitude and daily practice as opposed to a singular activity.

Mindfulness can be described as the capacity to maintain awareness of and a sense of openness to our current experience. In contrast to being preoccupied with negative thoughts about our past or worries about our future, mindfulness encourages us to fully attend to the present moment and to view ourselves and the world from a nonjudgmental, compassionate stance. Put simply, mindfulness is paying attention to the here and now.

Acceptance is an important component of mindfulness, which allows us to remain present during both unpleasant and pleasant emotions and experiences. The nonjudgmental aspect of mindfulness encourages us to stop using labels of "good" and "bad" in defining our experiences and situations but rather to simply be and observe.

Mindfulness is both incredibly simple and very challenging at the same time. It's not easy to quiet the mind, and survivors often feel especially anxious when left alone with their thoughts and memories. We can all begin our mindfulness practice by simply observing our present experience without defining, judging, or labeling. Whether that means observing our surroundings, our thoughts, our feelings, other people, or our sensations, as long as we remain in the present moment, we are being mindful. What becomes difficult is maintaining that neutral stance or attitude when our thoughts, feelings, or sensations begin to feel unpleasant or scary.

Like any new skill, the more you practice mindfulness the easier it becomes, and the more it will feel like a natural part of your life.

After you identify your automatic thought, ask yourself the following questions:

- Does this thought fall into any of the common problematic thought patterns?
- Is this thought extreme or exaggerated in any way?
- Is this thought helpful?

After you identify your behavior urge, ask yourself the following question:

- What are the consequences of this behavior?

EXERCISE: WATCHING YOUR THOUGHTS GO BY *(five to ten minutes)*

Instructions: Find a comfortable seated position. The first time you try this meditation, you may find that you are restless after only a few moments of sitting. Sit for as long as you feel able, then try again another time (and again after that). Aim to sit for a little longer each time. Like building a muscle, each time you try this meditation, you will be able to find inner stillness for a little bit longer.

- Take a deep breath in and exhale.
- Imagine that your mind is the sky and your thoughts are the clouds drifting by.
- Notice each thought as it drifts by, but don't hold on to it.
- Let it drift in and out of your mind.

Alternately:

- Take a deep breath in and exhale.
- Imagine that your thoughts are like the leaves floating down a stream of water.
- Watch each thought float by.
- Notice the pauses between each thought.
- Don't analyze or judge your thoughts, just watch them go.

EXERCISE: PROGRESSIVE MUSCLE RELAXATION

Instructions: Progressive muscle relaxation is a stress-reduction method that can be highly effective, especially if used regularly. The technique involves tensing or tightening one muscle group at a time, followed by a relaxation phase wherein you fully release the tension and pay close attention to the contrast. Move sequentially through your entire body, repeating this technique of tensing and relaxing. It is typical to begin with your extremities (your hands or feet/legs), but do whatever feels best or most natural to you.

1. Begin in a comfortable position (either sitting or lying down), ideally in a quiet room or space.
2. Take a deep breath in and contract one muscle group. Hold for five to ten seconds, and on the exhale release the tension.
3. Take a few moments to relax and notice the contrast you feel when your body is relaxed.
4. Move to the next muscle group, gradually working your way through your body, tensing and relaxing.
5. End with a few final deep breaths and a few moments of deep relaxation. Try to feel the heaviness of your body and let go of any remaining tension.

Example sequence:

- Make a fist with your hands and bend them back at the wrists. Then release.
- Bend your elbows and tense your biceps. Then release.
- Wrinkle your forehead as tightly as you can. Then release.
- Open your mouth wide and feel the tension in your jaw. Then release.
- Press your lips together and feel the tension in the back of your throat. Then release.
- Roll your head around your neck slowly, noticing the point of tension move as you do.
- Shrug your shoulders up toward your ears and hold. Then release.
- Tighten your stomach, tensing your abdominal muscles, and hold. Then release.
- Arch your back and notice the tension in your lower back. Then release.
- Tighten your buttocks and thighs. Then release.
- Straighten and tense your legs, curling your toes upward. Then release.

Trauma and the Tricks of Memory

Memory can be very fraught for trauma survivors. Whether it's because you're having difficulty recalling certain aspects of what happened or even having difficulty with retaining new memories, it can be frustrating and scary when you feel like you can't trust your own mind. To add to the complications, most trauma survivors experience intrusive memories and flashbacks that are not only distressing, but can also significantly impact their ability to concentrate or engage in normal daily activities, like work or socializing. It's not uncommon for trauma survivors to feel as though they are "losing control" or "losing their minds" due to the frequency and intensity of intrusive memories. The natural response is to avoid the memories or try to push them away. Unfortunately, attempts at avoidance often only make the intrusive memories worse.

A key to finding some peace and relief from your troubling memories lies in shifting from *intrusive* rumination to *deliberate* and *reflective* rumination. Your memories are going to come up one way or another. But when you reflect on them in a deliberate fashion, trying to think critically about what happened to you and your beliefs about it, you give yourself the opportunity to challenge errors in your thinking and eventually grow from the experience.

The best way to do this is to set time aside in your day to do nothing but focus on your thoughts and memories in a purposeful way. By consciously *choosing* to spend time with thoughts and memories, you'll likely decrease the number of intrusive memories and feel a greater sense of control over your mind. When unwanted thoughts and memories arise at other times during the day, you can remind yourself that you've set aside time to work through these memories and will come back to them in time. You may even choose to briefly document the thoughts and memories as they come up, to help inform your later reflection. All these strategies can help you manage your intrusive memories and thoughts and facilitate your healing and growth.

Memory Fragments and Blank Spots

Memory gaps are so common after trauma that the inability to recall aspects of what happened is recognized as a symptom of PTSD. Understanding how the brain reacts to life-threatening, dangerous, or emotionally overwhelming situations helps explain this common phenomenon. Imagine that you're being held at gunpoint. For obvious reasons, you would immediately become hyperfocused on the gun in your face. You'd pay little attention to the less relevant details of your surroundings, like the color of the assailant's hair or the clothes they're wearing. Later, you might find yourself unable to recall anything but the gun.

The object of this hyperfocus will vary in each traumatic context. For instance, it may be a stain on the wall that someone was forced to stare at while their head was pinned down during a rape. These things that the brain focuses on often become the content of your most painful and/or vivid flashbacks or intrusive memories.

What's happening is that the area of your brain that governs intentional control of attention (the prefrontal cortex) essentially shuts down during a traumatic event. Once the brain's fear circuitry takes over, it dictates where your attention goes. Typically, attention is either directed to a particular sensation, such as the sound of gunshots or the look on the predator's face, or to relatively meaningless details, like a flickering street lamp. Either way, it's typically fragmented and disorganized sensory information that gets stored as memories.

The fear circuit also impairs the hippocampus, which is responsible for encoding and storing information related to the sequence of time. This can result in trauma survivors having difficulty recalling the exact timeline or sequence of events, which unfortunately can cause further distress and complication, especially in legal contexts. I once worked with a survivor who'd been held hostage in a Latin American country for an extended period of time but had no concept of how much time had actually passed and could only vaguely describe how she spent her days.

If you were slipped a "date rape drug," such as Rohypnol or gamma hydroxybutyrate acid (GHB), or were otherwise intoxicated during the traumatic event, the trauma memory gaps may be even more significant, or your memory may be entirely absent. Regardless of the source or extent of your memory gaps, don't try to force yourself to remember aspects of the traumatic event that aren't readily available to you. Because of the brain's tendency to fill in memory gaps, this could result in inadvertently producing false or fabricated memories. Instead, focus on processing the aspects of your memories that are most vivid or distressing. In cases where there are significant memory lapses, focus on processing the peripheral memories, including the details of the last memories you have prior to going blank and the first memories following the gap.

EXERCISE: FACING THE HARDEST PART

Instructions: Think about the most vivid or distressing memory from your trauma experience. This may be a recurring flashback or image. Pick the memory that is causing you the most distress, even if it's only a partial description of what happened. In your notebook, describe this memory in detail, including as much sensory detail as possible (i.e., smells, sounds, images) and the emotions you felt or thoughts you had at the time.

Read the narrative aloud to yourself regularly (ideally daily, but at least weekly if this is more feasible for you) until there is a noticeable decrease in the amount of distress you experience in response to the memory. If you don't notice any improvement or find your level of distress worsening, it may be advisable to consult a trauma therapist for help confronting your memories in a supportive and safe environment. Ideally, when you set aside time to confront your most distressing memories, you'll notice a significant decrease in both the level of distress you experience in response to the memory and a decrease in the number of times you experience related intrusive memories or flashbacks.

Your Story, Part Two

At this point, you've already written in detail about what happened to you. You've also written out the most distressing memory (or memories) from the trauma you endured. The next step is to shift your focus away from *what* happened and begin to focus instead on the reasons *why* you believe the trauma happened and the *consequences* of the trauma for your thoughts and beliefs about yourself, others, and the world.

If you feel anxious about moving forward, examine your thoughts about that to see if you can catch any of your stuck points or a problematic thought pattern. For instance, if your first thought is that you may experience too many emotions and lose control, this may be one of your stuck points that you need to work through. And don't force yourself; take your time and be patient with the process. Any step is a step toward healing.

The following exercise will help you start to critically examine your thoughts and beliefs around the traumatic event, to help you move beyond the ideas that are keeping you stuck. If you've been struggling in the aftermath of your trauma for a long time, it may take some time to work through these issues and to sort out fact versus fiction. Again, the more willing you are to at least consider alternative ideas, the more likely you'll be able to shift toward a more balanced, flexible, and healthy way of thinking.

EXERCISE: THINKING CRITICALLY ABOUT WHAT HAPPENED TO YOU

In the space below, describe why you think the traumatic event happened to you:

What does the traumatic event mean to you?

How has the traumatic event changed the way you think about yourself?

How has the traumatic event changed the way you think about other people?

How has the traumatic event changed the way you think about the world or the "way things are"?

....

....

....

EXERCISE: IDENTIFYING YOUR INTERNAL TRIGGERS

Instructions: As you begin to think more critically about what happened to you, you may notice certain thoughts that evoke a particularly strong emotional reaction. For example, if there is a particular thought that brings tears to your eyes the moment you write it down or say it aloud, you've likely identified one of your internal triggers or "hot spots." Often these thoughts can also help you begin to identify a more deeply held (and perhaps even more painful) belief about yourself, others, or the world.

As with triggers generally, the more you're aware of which thoughts trigger you, the more control you have over your response to them. These are also good clues to reveal which beliefs or thought patterns you may need to spend more time examining.

Internal trigger thought:

....

....

....

Is this thought part of a more deeply held belief? If so, what belief does this thought represent?

....

....

....

Exercise continues to next page

Internal trigger thought:

_____

_____

_____

Is this thought part of a more deeply held belief? If so, what belief does this thought represent?

_____

_____

_____

Internal trigger thought:

_____

_____

_____

Is this thought part of a more deeply held belief? If so, what belief does this thought represent?

_____

_____

_____

What Do You Believe about What Happened to You?

It is typically easier to catch your faulty thinking about the trauma than to identify your more deeply held beliefs about what it means and why it happened to *you*. In general, the thoughts we have on a daily basis stem from an underlying belief system. The more ingrained that belief system is, the more it begins to feel *factual*. The more you become conscious of your thoughts and patterns in your thinking, the easier it will be to identify the beliefs that underlie them.

EXERCISE: BELIEFS ABOUT YOURSELF

Instructions: First consider how much your beliefs about yourself have changed since the traumatic event and then try to identify the beliefs that you currently hold. The beliefs that represent the most extreme shifts from your prior thinking are likely the ones you should spend the most time examining.

How much have your beliefs about yourself in the area of safety shifted since the traumatic event?

1	2	3	4	5	6	7	8	9	10

No Noticeable Change   Moderate Change   Dramatic Change

What beliefs do you currently hold about yourself and safety? (Example: I am not capable of keeping myself safe.)

_____

_____

_____

Exercise continues to next page

How much have your beliefs about yourself surrounding trust shifted since the trau-matic event?

1	2	3	4	5	6	7	8	9	10

No Noticeable Change · Moderate Change · Dramatic Change

What beliefs do you currently hold about yourself and trust? (Example: I can't trust people or I will get hurt.)

How much have your beliefs about yourself surrounding the notion of control shifted since the traumatic event?

1	2	3	4	5	6	7	8	9	10

No Noticeable Change · Moderate Change · Dramatic Change

What beliefs do you currently hold about yourself and control? (Example: I have no control over what happens to me.)

How much have your beliefs about yourself in the area of self-esteem shifted since the traumatic event?

```
   1        2        3        4        5        6        7        8        9        10
```

No Noticeable Change   Moderate Change   Dramatic Change

What beliefs do you currently hold about yourself in regard to your self-esteem? (Example: I am damaged; I am worthless.)

EXERCISE: BELIEFS ABOUT OTHER PEOPLE AND THE WORLD

Instructions: Repeat the exercise above, but this time instead of focusing on yourself, answer the same questions in regard to what you believe about other people and the world at large.

How much have your beliefs about others and the world shifted since the traumatic event in the area of safety?

```
   1        2        3        4        5        6        7        8        9        10
```

No Noticeable Change   Moderate Change   Dramatic Change

Exercise continues to next page

What beliefs do you currently hold about others and the world in regard to safety?
(Example: The world is not a safe place.)

1	2	3	4	5	6	7	8	9	10

No Noticeable Change   Moderate Change   Dramatic Change

How much have your beliefs about others and the world shifted since the traumatic event in
the area of trust?

1	2	3	4	5	6	7	8	9	10

No Noticeable Change   Moderate Change   Dramatic Change

What beliefs do you currently hold about others and the world in regard to trust?
(Example: It is dangerous to trust people.)

1	2	3	4	5	6	7	8	9	10

No Noticeable Change   Moderate Change   Dramatic Change

How much have your beliefs about others and the world shifted since the traumatic event in
the area of power and control?

1	2	3	4	5	6	7	8	9	10

No Noticeable Change   Moderate Change   Dramatic Change

What beliefs do you currently hold about others and the world in regard to power and control? (Example: The people in power have all the control.)

1	2	3	4	5	6	7	8	9	10

No Noticeable Change   Moderate Change   Dramatic Change

How much have your beliefs about others and the world shifted since the traumatic event in the area of intimacy?

1	2	3	4	5	6	7	8	9	10

No Noticeable Change   Moderate Change   Dramatic Change

What beliefs do you currently hold about others and the world in regard to intimacy? (Example: If I let my guard down, I will get hurt.)

1	2	3	4	5	6	7	8	9	10

No Noticeable Change   Moderate Change   Dramatic Change

EXERCISE: CHALLENGING OLD BELIEFS WITH NEW POSSIBILITIES

> *Note: You may want to photocopy this worksheet so you can repeat the process for multiple beliefs.*

List one belief that has shifted dramatically since the traumatic event:

_____

_____

_____

How deeply held is this belief (from 0% to 100%)? _____

CHALLENGING QUESTIONS:

What is the evidence for this belief?

_____

_____

_____

What is the evidence against this belief?

_____

_____

_____

Is this belief extreme or exaggerated in any way? (Does it include any extreme words that could be modified like always, never, should, *or* everyone?*)*

....

....

....

Is this belief based more on feelings than facts?

....

....

....

Is this belief helpful to you? Or making you feel better?

....

....

....

Is this belief in line with your values (or what is important to you)?

....

....

....

Exercise continues to next page

New belief/way of thinking:

_____

_____

_____

How much do you believe in this new belief/way of thinking (from 0% to 100%)? _____

A New Story

You can't rewrite history or change what happened to you, but you can absolutely rewrite the stories that you tell yourself going forward. In other words, you are likely not the reason this horrible thing happened to you, but you *will* be the reason you learn to flourish and move forward. As we saw previously, research shows that there are three possible eventual outcomes following a traumatic event: (1) psychological distress/disorder, (2) return to baseline, and (3) posttraumatic growth.

As we have discussed, those who experience posttraumatic growth are often the individuals who have been able to *deliberately* reflect on what happened, as opposed to those who have passively endured the constant barrage of intrusive thoughts and memories. The areas of posttraumatic growth most commonly discussed include recognition of one's personal strength and resilience, improved relationships, a deeper appreciation of life, an awareness of new life paths and possibilities, spiritual changes, and a new understanding of life's meaning and purpose. Consider these potential areas of growth as you begin writing your new story.

EXERCISE: WRITING A NEW STORY

Instructions: Using a notebook or piece of paper, write the account of your traumatic event again. However, this time, add your comments about your current thoughts, feelings, and interpretations of the events in parentheses as you go along. For instance, you may add a comment like "I realize now that I could not control what happened to me," or "I still feel sad when I think about this," or "I stopped trusting people for a long time, but I am working on reconnecting with others."

EXERCISE: ACTION PLAN FOR RESPONDING TO STUCK POINTS

Instructions: Select all of the following strategies that you are willing to engage in order to begin to identify and shift your stuck points:

☐ Keep a log or record of all the stuck points I identify.

☐ Examine my stuck points to see if they fall into one of the categories of common problematic thought patterns.

☐ Critically examine the evidence for or against my stuck points.

☐ Maintain an attitude of willing exploration when examining my thoughts and beliefs surrounding the traumatic event.

☐ Use mindfulness or relaxation strategies when a stuck point evokes a difficult emotion or sensation.

☐ Try to connect my stuck points to the underlying beliefs I hold about myself, others, and the world.

☐ Take time to *deliberately* reflect upon what happened to me and what it means.

☐ _____

☐ _____

What will progress look like to me?

....

....

....

....

....

Chapter Takeaways

In this chapter you explored your thoughts and beliefs surrounding a traumatic event and how your thought patterns may have shifted since the trauma. You should now have:

- An understanding of common problematic thought patterns.
- An initial sense (at least) of the specific thoughts and beliefs that may be holding you back in your recovery.
- Some tools to begin challenging any distorted or unhealthy thinking you may be engaging in.
- Several ways to break the link between your thoughts and unhealthy or unhelpful behaviors.
- The ability to critically examine the beliefs you hold surrounding what happened to you.
- New, more balanced ways of thinking about what happened to you and what it means about yourself, others, and the world.

CHAPTER 4

Your Body

What You'll Learn in This Chapter

This chapter will cover how trauma impacts your body, including the association between trauma and elevated stress levels, which can result in stress-related symptoms and illnesses. You will begin to learn how to listen to your body, even when it hurts, and you may begin connecting some of your symptoms and/or sensations to your traumatic experience. You will also learn tools for reconnecting to your body and developing a greater sense of relaxation and sensory awareness.

The chapter also covers some strategies to help you assess and manage sleep disruptions, which are all too familiar to trauma survivors. Finally, we'll cover the importance of nutrition and physical activity in reaching optimal health and wellness, and other healing self-care habits.

My hope for you is to finish this chapter with a better sense of your strengths and challenges in this area and a deeper connection to your body and what it may be trying to communicate to you. You will also have the opportunity to develop some concrete goals for wellness habits to incorporate in your life.

Where the Brain Goes, the Body Follows

Trauma impacts your entire being—mind, brain, and body. Changes that occur throughout your nervous system and brain in the aftermath of a traumatic event can result in a wide range of physical symptoms and diseases, such as chronic fatigue and autoimmune conditions like arthritis, lupus, and type 2 diabetes.

The brain develops our more primitive functions first, before it develops the areas associated with higher thinking. Our "reptilian brain" is the first to develop and is responsible for basic functions like eating, sleeping, breathing, and feeling things like hunger, temperature, and pain.

The "mammalian brain" develops next. This includes our limbic system, which has been called the *seat of emotion*. The limbic system controls emotions like fear, anger, and sadness and determines whether incoming stimuli should be interpreted as pleasurable or threatening.

The neocortex is the top layer of our frontal lobe and the last area of the brain to develop. The neocortex helps us articulate things through language, plan and reflect, control our impulses, and understand abstract and symbolic concepts.

When our brains sense danger, the higher order parts shut down, and the more primitive systems take over, propelling us to run, hide, or fight, aka *fight or flight*. For example, if you're home alone at night and see a sudden movement out of the corner of your eye, your body may lurch into an immediate fear response. Your heart starts racing, and your system floods with adrenaline—*before* the logical part of your brain kicks in and reminds you that the fan is in the window, blowing the curtains. Similarly, if you're experiencing a flashback, the primitive parts of your brain can't really distinguish a memory from a current experience. In response to the perceived danger, the brain will activate a host of physical symptoms (such as racing heart, sweating, or shortness of breath) long before the neocortex comes online to remind you that you're not actually experiencing a live threat.

Trauma increases the likelihood that we will misinterpret threats. We become more likely to assume situations are dangerous, and we react accordingly. Research studies have demonstrated that when a survivor hears a script recounting the details of their traumatic event or otherwise reexperiences it, the same physiological response is activated as if the event were actually occurring. This frequent reactivation of the fight-or-flight response depletes our bodies' resources, leading to numerous physical symptoms or ailments over time.

In daily life, this tendency to misinterpret threats might also manifest as relationship difficulties. For example, a trauma survivor would be more likely assume that the slightest grimace on the face of a loved one signals impending abandonment and may respond by lashing out or by quietly increasing distance from the relationship.

One of the main reasons trauma is so difficult to talk about is that when you recall what happened, your body reexperiences the sensations of the fight-or-flight response (such as a racing heartbeat) as well as the feelings of terror or helplessness you experienced at the time of the original event. Structural and functional brain changes associated with trauma exposure and PTSD further explain why recalling and retelling your experience can feel unbearable. Studies have found that during the reexperiencing of a traumatic event, the area of the brain known as the speech center is significantly deactivated, whereas the region of the cortex that registers and processes visual information exhibits heightened activation. This is why a reminder of your trauma can trigger a vivid mental image of what happened (i.e., a flashback), but you may still have difficulty putting the experience into words.

When a traumatic experience is too overwhelming to process, our memory can become increasingly split and fragmented. Sensory memories (such as smells and/or sounds) that were haphazardly encoded in our brains during the trauma start to intrude on the present (in the form of a flashback). This often leads people to become hyperaware of anything that may remind them of their trauma and increase their attempts to avoid such stimuli. In turn, this can result in a sense of alienation from your body and/or a tendency to ignore your physical needs as a way to avoid difficult sensations. In fact, research shows that trauma survivors are less likely to engage in preventive health behaviors, such as maintaining regular physical activity, eating a healthy diet, and engaging in routine medical screening. The skills and exercises discussed in this chapter will help you begin to heal the mind-body rift your trauma may have created.

The Long-Term Physical Impact of Stress

Chronic stress impacts your long-term physical health because your body is sustaining the prolonged release of stress hormones and other chemicals that result from the fight-or-flight response. The autonomic nervous system (ANS), a network of nerves that originates in the spinal cord and communicates with all of the organs, plays a major role here. There are two branches of the ANS—the *sympathetic* ANS and the *parasympathetic* ANS. The fight-or-flight response is initiated within the sympathetic ANS. If this system remains on high alert for an extended period of time, either due to actually facing chronic danger (war zones, dangerous neighborhoods, abusive relationships) or frequently *perceiving* danger (such as frequent flashbacks or other physiological reactions to trauma reminders), you become vulnerable to stress-related illnesses.

Problems like muscle tension and headaches are often a direct response to stress, and a host of other illnesses are exacerbated by chronic stress. The good news is that many of these stress-related symptoms can be resolved with changes in how you care for yourself, including developing some skills to combat your exaggerated stress reactions.

EXERCISE: STRESS INVENTORY

Instructions: To help you begin to identify how much stress you experience daily, answer the following questions:

How many signs of excess stress (listed below) do you experience regularly? ____

	YES	NO
Do you frequently experience a stiff neck or back pain?		
Are you easily irritated?		
Do you have difficulty falling or staying asleep?		
Do you grind your teeth?		
Do you often feel tired, regardless of how much you slept?		
Do you frequently feel overwhelmed or under pressure?		
Do you have recurrent stomachaches?		
Do you have recurrent headaches?		
Do you have difficulty concentrating?		
Are you often concerned with what other people are thinking about you?		
Do you often worry about money/your finances?		
Do you regularly use tobacco, alcohol, or other drugs to help you relax?		
Do you find yourself distracted or otherwise unable to enjoy activities that should be pleasurable?		
Do you often feel tense?		
Do you get sick often?		
Do you often feel anxious, with no identified cause?		
Do you continually worry about things in the future?		
Do you find yourself "snapping" or otherwise lashing out at other people?		
Do you have trouble remembering things?		
Do you experience your heart pounding frequently?		

Everyone experiences some stress-related symptoms. However, if you answered yes to many or most of the questions above, you're likely experiencing high levels of stress, and it will be important for you develop skills and strategies to reduce it.

Now that you're familiar with your typical signs of stress, I encourage you to pay attention to your stress levels throughout the week and see if you can identify some of your sources of stress.

Once you've identified the people and/or situations that increase your stress levels, try to make adjustments to accommodate this by practicing exercises we've discussed previously like mindfulness (page 39) or progressive muscle relaxation (page 54). Always begin by taking a deep breath (or three), in through your nose and out with an open mouth, whenever you begin to sense your stress levels rising. This helps communicate to your nervous system that you are not facing actual danger and reduces the chance that your body will engage in a fight-or-flight reaction.

Substance Abuse

It is very common for an individual who has experienced a traumatic event to initiate substance use or to increase their use of substances to a problematic degree. The relationship between trauma and substance abuse appears to be particularly strong for women. Studies have estimated that the rate of co-occurring PTSD and substance use is between 12 and 34 percent for men and 30 and 59 percent for women. Both trauma *and* substance abuse make individuals more vulnerable to repeated trauma or abuse, so the combination of the two can be particularly dangerous. Further, actively using substances makes trauma treatment less effective (and vice versa).

The relationship between substance abuse and PTSD makes intuitive sense. When someone is suffering, either physically or mentally, it is natural to find ways to alleviate or even "numb" our pain. John Briere, a psychiatrist and scientist, has termed this phenomenon the *pain paradox*: in trying to reduce painful or upsetting states,

traumatized or otherwise suffering people inadvertently engage in behaviors that sustain or enhance their pain.

If you are engaging in problematic substance use, there are many ways to seek help. *Seeking Safety* is a specific treatment modality developed by Lisa Najavits to treat co-occurring PTSD and substance abuse. This treatment, which is often offered in a group setting, focuses on establishing physical and mental safety, learning how to detach from emotional pain without substances, finding meaning in your life, and developing healthy support systems. For a list of providers across the United States that offer *Seeking Safety*, go to Treatment-Innovations.org /locate-ss.html. The Substance Abuse and Mental Health Administration (SAMHSA) also has a National Helpline that offers a free, confidential, 24/7, 365-days-a-year treatment referral and information service (in English and Spanish) for individuals and families facing mental and/or substance use disorders.

Chronic Symptoms and Illnesses

Trauma exposure and PTSD are associated with increased rates of medically unexplained symptoms, such as dizziness, ringing in the ears (*tinnitus*), and blurry vision as well as a wide range of medical conditions, including cardiovascular, respiratory, musculoskeletal, neurological, and gastrointestinal disorders as well as diabetes and chronic pain.

The complex somatic symptoms and conditions associated with trauma exposure and PTSD are likely the result of several stress-related processes, some of which we've already discussed. Muscle tension is a natural, reactive response to stress in an effort to protect ourselves. But when the muscles remain in a nearly constant state of tension, this can result in chronic pain and can trigger other reactions in the body that may lead to stress-related illnesses. Similarly, during the fight-or-flight response, stress hormones send signals to the body that result in increased heart rate and stronger contractions of the heart muscles. If it's not addressed, chronic activation of the stress response can lead to increased risk of hypertension, heart attack, and stroke.

EXERCISE: PAIN ASSESSMENT

Instructions: Using the images below, circle any areas of your body where you are currently experiencing or have recently experienced pain. Use a darker circle (or different color) to indicate areas of intense pain versus a lighter circle (or alternate color) to indicate areas of dull or mild pain.

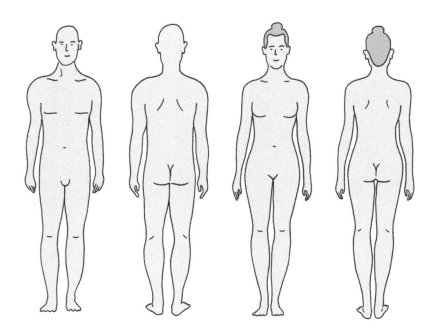

After you've identified all the areas of pain in your body, consider your next steps for healing.

- For areas of intense, persistent pain, consider seeking medical attention to begin to address these issues.
- For areas of more dull or mild pain, see if you can work with this pain using relaxation strategies. Take a deep breath and visualize your breath reaching this specific area of your body; repeat until you feel at least a mild sense of relief. Tense this area of your body and then release the tension to begin to work on relaxing your muscles. When you experience the pain, try to be mindful of any muscle tension you may be holding, and release it when possible.

Talking to Your Doctor about Trauma

Discussing your trauma is not an easy thing to do. But it can be very helpful to alert your doctor to what you have been through in order to receive sensitive, trauma-informed care and to help your doctor make potentially crucial connections between your physical and psychological symptoms and the trauma you experienced.

Preparation for this conversation can start before you enter the doctor's office. To begin, consider if you have a gender or ethnicity preference for your doctor. For a woman who was sexually assaulted by a male perpetrator, receiving gynecological care from a man may be more uncomfortable. Consider bringing a close friend or family member to your appointment if that will make you feel more comfortable. Some people prefer to bring a written statement of what happened to them, a checklist of symptoms, or a list of questions to their appointments in order to reduce the amount they actually have

to talk about it. The US Department of Veterans Affairs's National Center for PTSD provides a helpful checklist of PTSD symptoms and common physical symptoms related to trauma exposure that you may find useful in preparing for your doctor's visit (www.PTSD.VA.gov/public /assessment/trauma-symptom-checklist.asp).

There may also be a simple request you could make of your doctor that would help make your visits more comfortable. For example, I worked with a client who experienced flashbacks and physiological reactions when she was placed fully on her back at the dentist's office, as it was a harsh reminder of the position she was held in during a gang rape. She requested that she complete her dental work in a more upright position and was able to receive much-needed dental work without being triggered. Remember that doctors are trained to discuss sensitive and embarrassing topics with you and are usually able to do so in a professional way.

Mind-Body Healing

During my first session with a teenage client I'll call Christine, I could see immediately that she felt uncomfortable in her own skin. Although dressed impeccably in stylish clothing, her presentation was anything but confident. She was hunched over, with both her legs and arms crossed, almost to the point of being curled into a twisted ball. She did not make any eye contact when she spoke but rather stared vacantly at the ground. Her foot was anxiously tapping the ground, while one of her hands bounced repeatedly on her leg. She quickly made it clear that she did not want to be in therapy and barely wanted to talk; she'd come at the urging of her parents, whom she clearly cared for and did not want to upset further.

In learning more about Christine, I discovered that she was born in an overcrowded Russian orphanage and was likely severely deprived of physical contact and basic nutrients as an infant. She'd been recently raped by an older male acquaintance and had since started cutting herself. Despite attempts to keep her away from any sharp objects, her parents had resorted to conducting body checks in order to identify the areas of her body she had most recently cut. Self-harm, in the form of cutting, is a common symptom for individuals experiencing a severe mind-body split—the emotional pain becomes so overwhelming that physical pain provides a welcome distraction. For many, it's the only way to break through the numbness and disconnection they feel from their bodies.

Christine was much more willing to engage in nonverbal exercises. We began with a simple mindfulness exercise of deep breathing and letting the mind gently observe her passing thoughts as if they were clouds floating by, without judgment or attachment. Mindfulness practices typically begin with setting up a physical posture to allow the breath to flow more freely throughout your body. I often describe this posture to clients as a "dignified posture." To begin, you place both feet firmly on the ground. Next, sit up straight and, with your shoulders slightly back and your head held high, gaze straight ahead. With tears in her eyes Christine reluctantly followed my instructions for getting into this posture. When she did, it felt like I was witnessing an extreme transformation before my eyes. Despite the tears, she immediately looked less sad, less vulnerable, and less vacant. I could begin to see her inhabiting her body.

After a traumatic experience, the sense of helplessness you felt is often stored in your memory systems as muscle tension or a feeling of disconnection from the areas of your body that may have been affected. Trauma survivors can become experts in numbing unwanted sensory experiences. This might take the form of abusing pain medications or alcohol, overeating, or becoming overly controlled in what you consume. Alternatively, you could become so focused on work or school that you disconnect entirely from your physical being. On the flip side, others may seek extreme sensations to counter the numbness they feel so strongly. For Christine, this came in the form of cutting. For others it might be engaging in promiscuous sex or reckless driving. My clients often say this type of risk taking is the only way they can feel *anything*; it can also give them the false sense that they're now in control of their pain.

Because the trauma survivor's innate alarm system is working on overdrive, it's crucial to reconnect mind and body in order to calm the overactive nervous system. Mindfulness practices, like taking a deep breath and calmly observing your thoughts and emotions, give your brain more time to activate its higher-level functions, which help you organize information in a logical manner.

The following exercises are meant to help you begin to reconnect with your body without needing to resort to extreme sensation seeking or numbing tactics. I have had many clients who tell me that the first time they try to do something like an audio-guided meditation, they can get through about one to five seconds before being overcome by an overwhelming sense of anxiety or emotional discomfort, and they abandon the activity altogether. That is to be expected, and it's okay to start slowly.

Think of building up your mindfulness skills like you'd build a muscle. The more you practice, the stronger you become. You may start with only a brief moment of guided meditation or one yoga or tai chi posture. Hopefully, the next time you return to your practice, you'll be able to sustain *two* seconds or postures. The trick is simply returning and trying again. And again, and again. There is now ample research showing that mind-body practices like yoga and breath retraining exercises have dramatic effects on psychological symptoms, like depression and anxiety, as well as positive impacts on a wide range of medical problems, including high blood pressure, stress-related illnesses, and chronic pain.

EXERCISE: BODY SCAN MEDITATION

Instructions: The following exercise can be done sitting in a chair or lying down on a firm surface. If sitting, maintain an upright posture, with your feet firmly on the ground. Close your eyes, if that is comfortable to you.

1. Begin by taking a few deep breaths. Try to bring your awareness to your body.
2. As you inhale, envision bringing oxygen to every part of your body, from the center of your being out to your extremities.
3. As you exhale, envision yourself relaxing more fully and deeply with each breath.
4. As we go through the scan of your body from your toes moving upward, notice any tension you are holding. When you notice tension, exaggerate it slightly by tensing the muscles more strongly and then releasing, allowing yourself to relax fully.
5. Start your body scan by noticing your feet. If you are sitting, observe the sensation of your feet touching the floor. Notice the weight and pressure of your feet on the ground. If you are not sitting, notice whatever sensation or vibrations you may feel in your feet.
6. Now shift your attention to your legs. Notice the weight of your legs on the floor or against the chair. Notice any pressure or pulsing, any heaviness or lightness.
7. Bring your attention to your back. Notice the pressure of your back against the floor or chair.
8. Now bring your attention to your stomach. You can place your hand on your stomach while you take a deep breath in. Is your stomach tense or tight? Let it soften as you exhale and release any tension.
9. Notice your hands. See if you can allow your fingers to uncurl and soften.
10. Next, move your attention to your arms. Feel any sensations in your arms and then release as fully as you can.
11. Notice your shoulders. Let them be soft and relaxed.
12. Bring your attention to your neck. Move your neck gently to release any tension.
13. Notice your jaw and your facial muscles. Let them be soft.
14. Take a deep breath and shift your awareness to your entire body. As you inhale, envision bringing oxygen to every part of your body, from the center of your being out to your extremities. As you exhale, envision relaxing more fully and deeply with each breath.
15. When you are ready, blink your eyes softly open.

Instructions: The following movements are intended to be done slowly, in order to help you breathe deeply and clear your mind. If your mind wanders, gently release your thoughts and return to focusing on your physical movements and the in and out of your breath.

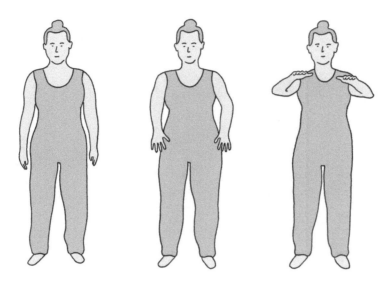

1. Stand comfortably, with your feet shoulder width apart (your knees can be slightly bent).
2. Relax your shoulders and lift your head slightly, so that your chin is up, with your eyes gazing straight ahead.
3. Your arms should hang comfortably by your sides, with your palms facing back.
4. As you take a deep breath in, raise your arms to shoulder width and height (your elbows can be slightly bent).
5. With your exhale, lower your arms slowly until they rest again comfortably by your side.
6. Repeat as many times as you would like.

EXERCISE: ALTERNATE NOSTRIL BREATHING *(Pranayama)*

This exercise brings your full focus to your breath, as you breathe "in one side and out the other." It has the added benefit of giving your mind something to do while your breath does its calming work.

1. Begin seated comfortably, with your legs crossed and an upright posture.
2. Bring your left thumb and ring finger together to touch and place your hand on your left knee, with your palm facing upward. (In yoga, when your fingers touch in such a way, it is called a mudra, which means "seal" or "closure" in Sanskrit.)
3. Rest the index and second finger of your right hand on your forehead.
4. Gently close your right nostril with your thumb.
5. Inhale deeply through your left nostril.
6. Now close your left nostril with your ring finger while opening your right nostril by removing your thumb.
7. Exhale slowly through your right nostril.
8. Inhale through your right nostril, with your fingers remaining in the same position.
9. Close your right nostril with your thumb while simultaneously releasing your finger from your left nostril.
10. Exhale through your left nostril.
11. Begin the next cycle by inhaling through your left nostril, with your fingers in the same position.
12. Continue alternating through each cycle for as long as you wish and ideally until you feel a sense of calm.

The Healing Power of Sleep

Adequate sleep is truly fundamental to both physical and mental well-being. While we sleep, both our bodies and our brains recover and regenerate. Particularly during *slow-wave sleep*, our tissues and cells repair themselves, and brain chemical and hormone levels are balanced out. In fact, when laboratory rats are deprived of slow-wave sleep for several days, their brains begin to malfunction, and they become physically sick. Humans react in much the same way. If you think back to the last time you had a few nights of poor sleep, you will likely remember feeling confused, achy, and emotional. Getting a good night's sleep is critical to our overall health and wellness.

Unfortunately, sleep disturbances are very common for trauma survivors. Nightmares and difficulties falling and/or staying asleep are core features of PTSD. You may fall asleep easily only to be awoken each night drenched in sweat, with your heart pounding, after having a vivid nightmare related to the trauma you endured. Or you could experience nightmares that feel like flashbacks. Others may experience difficulty falling asleep in the first place. You may feel exhausted during the day, but the moment you lay your head on your pillow, your mind goes into overdrive with difficult memories or worries from your day.

Developing good sleep habits is an important part of healing. Be open to trying different strategies until you find a routine that works for you, and then *stick with it*. Consistency is key. If you continue to experience persistent sleep difficulties, it may be helpful to consult a psychiatrist or physician about receiving a pharmaceutical sleep aid, ideally one that is not habit-forming. Be sure to talk to your doctor about the risks and side effects of any medication you decide to take.

Although there's some evidence of slight individual variability regarding how much sleep someone needs, the general rule of thumb is eight hours per night for optimal well-being (or seven to nine hours). According to recent Gallup polls, the average American is currently getting only 6.8 hours per night, suggesting that most of us are at least somewhat chronically sleep deprived.

Most Americans ingest caffeine daily in efforts to combat the effects of this loss of sleep. For many people eight hours of sleep per night might seem unrealistic based on the demands of work or other life responsibilities. It's important to try to make sleep a top priority. It may be helpful to remind yourself that adequate sleep will improve your efficiency, in essence making your waking hours more productive.

EXERCISE: SLEEP DISRUPTION ASSESSMENT

Instructions: Answer the following questions in order to identify your sleep patterns and typical sources of sleep disruption.

If you are seeking medical assistance for your sleep disruptions, this information can be helpful to share with your medical professional.

1. How many nights of the week do you experience sleep disruptions? _____
2. What is your typical bedtime? _____
3. What is your typical wake time? _____
4. What is your average number of restful sleep hours each night? _____
5. Is your sleep-wake cycle relatively consistent?   Yes ☐   No ☐
6. Do you sleep in on weekends?   Yes ☐   No ☐
7. Do you nap during the day?   Yes ☐   No ☐
8. Do you drink caffeine each morning?   Yes ☐   No ☐
9. Do you drink alcohol in the evenings?   Yes ☐   No ☐
10. Do you wait to go to bed until you feel drowsy?   Yes ☐   No ☐
11. Do you dim the lights or shut the curtains to reduce bright light shortly before your bedtime?   Yes ☐   No ☐
12. Do you lower the temperature before going to bed?   Yes ☐   No ☐
13. Do you frequently engage in activities in your bed aside from sleep, such as reading, watching television, or searching the Internet on your phone?   Yes ☐   No ☐
14. Do you experience the most difficulty falling asleep?   Yes ☐   No ☐
    a. *If yes, do you lay in bed for longer than fifteen minutes trying to fall asleep?*   Yes ☐   No ☐
    b. *Is one of the reasons you can't fall asleep worry or anxiety?*   Yes ☐   No ☐
    c. *Is one of the reasons you can't fall asleep a vague feeling of restlessness?*   Yes ☐   No ☐
    d. *Do you start to stress about how much sleep you are going to get when you can't fall asleep?*   Yes ☐   No ☐
15. Do you experience the most difficulty staying asleep?   Yes ☐   No ☐
    a. *If yes, do you experience nightmares?*   Yes ☐   No ☐
    b. *How many times do you typically wake up throughout the night?* _____
    c. *How long does it typically take you to fall back asleep?* _____

How to Get Healthy Sleep

As summarized by Dr. Ilardi in his book *The Depression Cure*, the following healthy sleep habits have been found to be effective in combating insomnia and other sleep difficulties:

1. Use your bed only for sleep (or sex).
   - In essence, you want to condition your body to associate your bed with sleeping.
   - If you have been lying awake for more than fifteen minutes, get out of bed and ideally leave your bedroom. Do something relaxing, such as reading a book or engaging in guided meditation, until you feel drowsy again. This helps reverse the cycle of lying in bed fretting about how much difficulty you are having falling asleep, which often serves only to make you increasingly anxious.

2. Don't get in bed until you feel drowsy.
   - Although you may initially feel anxious to get to bed in order to get the most possible sleep, if you are consistently having difficulty falling asleep, you want to wait to get in bed until you are feeling sufficiently sleepy.
   - Avoid doing any stimulating activities before bed, including work or exercise.
   - Even if you already have a nightly routine that seems to make you feel drowsy, like reading in bed prior to falling asleep, try moving this activity out of the bed and the bedroom. The exception to this is sexual activity, which research has shown does not dampen the sleep-bed conditioning process.

3. Wake up at the same time each day and go to sleep at the same time each night.
   - The brain has a built-in "sleep meter" that ultimately sets your sleep drive and makes you feel drowsiness (or not). When this system is in balance, you typically begin to feel tired around the same time each night. When it is not functioning in balance, you can help rebalance the system by setting a consistent wake-sleep routine.
   - This means that you try to resist the temptation to sleep in on the weekends, although you can make more exceptions once you have successfully established a good sleep routine.

> *Note: If you are working on the first two steps, this would be the exception to trying to get to bed at the same time.*

4. Avoid taking naps.
   - When you nap, you reduce your sleep drive and will likely be less tired when it is time to go to bed.

5. Avoid drinking caffeine, especially after noon.
   - Caffeine reduces your brain's sleep drive.

6. Avoid alcohol at night.
   - Although many people find that alcohol, like a glass of wine in the evening, can help them feel drowsy, there is a rebound effect that results in restlessness, poor sleep quality, and late-night awakening.

7. Avoid bright light at night.
   - Bright indoor light can trick our bodies into thinking it is daytime.

8. Lower the temperature.
   - There is some evidence that a drop in temperature can increase the sleep drive (and therefore your sense of drowsiness).

9. Don't worry!
   - Don't worry about *not* falling asleep.
   - Turn the clock away from you so you do not stress about what time it is/how little sleep you are going to get.
   - As much as you can, avoid thinking about anything negative when trying to fall asleep.
   - Use the coping strategies you have learned throughout this book (see chapters 2 and 3 for reminders of strategies related to dealing with difficult thoughts and emotions).
   - Some people find it helpful to write down their worries before bed, as a way to release them. Others like to take this a step further by then folding or ripping the paper to symbolically represent releasing the thoughts.
   - Try to focus your attention on positive thoughts and images.
   - Engage in diaphragmatic breathing.

Sleep Meditations

Guided-Audio Sleep Meditations

Many people find that audio recordings are the most helpful form of sleep meditations. The following are a few sample resources:

- MARC.UCLA.edu/mindful-meditations

See specifically Body Scan for Sleep.

- Equinox.com/meditation

Six meditations under the sleep section.

- iTunes.Apple.com/us/app
/relax-with-andrew-johnson
/id303609195?mt=8

Customizable sleep and relaxation recordings.

- Meditainment.com/meditation-for
-falling-asleep

A free resource with guided meditation and calming audio.

- Headspace.com

A subscription service that provides access to a large guided meditation library, including sleep meditations.

EXERCISE: MEDITATION: VISUALIZE A SAFE SPACE

Instructions: The following guided meditation is intended to help you create a rich visual space that you find safe and peaceful in. You can record yourself reading this script and listen to it as you do this, or simply read it once and follow the basic guidelines of visualizing a safe space in your mind (Note: If you are recording the script, try to read it at a steady pace and in a calm voice).

Some people base their visualization on a familiar place from their real lives that they associate with happy memories, such as a favorite beach, home, or hiking trail. Others use their imaginations to create their safe spaces.

The more sensory detail you are able to add, such as sights, sounds, feelings, and scents, the richer and more engrossing the visualization will become. Typically, the more you return to this image, the stronger it becomes and the more you are able to utilize it during times of distress.

To go to your safe space, lie down and close your eyes. Let your arms lie softly by your sides, with your palms facing upward. Try to completely let go of any tension you are holding in your body. Take a deep breath. As you exhale, release any remaining tension.

Walk slowly to your safe space. Your space can be inside or outdoors; it just needs to be peaceful and calm.

As you walk toward your safe space either via path or entrance, notice the sights and sounds around you.

Feel your worries and tension lift with each step you take.

Notice the view in the distance.

Notice what is right in front of you. How does it smell? How do you feel? What do you hear?

Arrive at your favorite place within your safe space. Be safe here. Sit or lie down in your safe space. Again, what do you see? How does it feel?

Reach out and touch something within your safe space. What is the texture? How does it feel?

Nothing can harm you here. Relax. Take a deep breath. Try to stay here calmly for a few moments. Memorize this place. The smells, sights, and sounds. Say a positive affirmation to yourself, like, "I am calm here," "All is well here," or "I am okay." You can come back here anytime you want.

Leave on the same path or through the same entrance by which you came. Again, notice the sights, smells, and sounds around you. Appreciate the view in the distance.

When you are ready, gently blink your eyes open.

EXERCISE: A NEW ROUTINE *(Planning for Sleep Disruptions)*

Instructions: Identify three new healthy sleep habits, and commit to trying each strategy consistently for a minimum of seven days/nights.

1. ....

2. ....

3. ....

Exercise continues to next page

If you are having difficulty identifying where to start, review your answers to the Sleep Disruption Assessment and review the section of this chapter on healthy sleep habits (page 85). Use the following cheat sheet to identify the strategies that may be most helpful to you:

CHEAT SHEET	
If you answered **no** to question 5	see healthy sleep habit #3
If you answered **yes** to question 6	see healthy sleep habit #3
If you answered **yes** to question 7	see healthy sleep habit #4
If you answered **yes** to question 8	see healthy sleep habit #5
If you answered **yes** to question 9	see healthy sleep habit #6
If you answered **no** to question 10	see healthy sleep habit #2
If you answered **no** to question 11	see healthy sleep habit #7
If you answered **no** to question 12	see healthy sleep habit #8
If you answered **yes** to question 13	see healthy sleep habit #1
If you answered **yes** to question 14a	see healthy sleep habit #1
If you answered **yes** to question 14b	see healthy sleep habit #9
If you answered **yes** to question 14c	try engaging in daily regular exercise
If you answered **yes** to question 14d	see healthy sleep habit #9
If you answered **yes** to question 15a	try engaging in deep breathing, listen to an audio sleep meditation, use the safe space visualization, or sing or listen to calming music
If your answer to question 15c is longer than fifteen minutes	see healthy sleep habit #1

Instructions: Track your nightly hours of restful sleep during the week you try these strategies:

Monday: _____

Tuesday: _____

Wednesday: _____

Thursday: _____

Friday: _____

Saturday: _____

Sunday: _____

Add up the total hours of sleep: _____

Divide by 7 to calculate your weekly average: _____ .

Is this weekly average better or worse than your typical sleep average (question 4 on your Sleep Disruption Assessment)?

If it is better, keep at it! You are on the right track.

If the amount you slept is about the same or below your typical average, try three new strategies for a week and follow the same tracking pattern. Keep at it until you find a routine that works for you.

EXERCISE: STARTING A DREAM JOURNAL

Instructions: Use the following format to record memorable dreams and to begin tracking recurrent themes or patterns from your dreams. Once you identify recurrent themes, it can help you gain valuable psychological insight about yourself and/or help you identify points of fear or pain that it may be helpful to work through. Some people keep a paper and writing utensil by their bed in order to jot down memorable notes from their dreams in the middle of the night (don't use this strategy if it disrupts your sleep). You can also try using a voice recorder to recount the details of your dream (preferably using a dedicated device so you aren't disturbed by the light of your phone).

Otherwise, record the details of your dreams first thing in the morning when they are the freshest.

Date: _____

Description of dream (add as many details as you can, even if they seem irrelevant at the time):

....

....

....

Is this a recurrent dream?

☐ Yes   ☐ No

Identify any themes or patterns from this dream:

....

....

....

Nourishing the Body and Mind

By the time I met Patricia, her weight was too high to be measured on a traditional scale. She walked with the assistance of a walker, and even then she had to stop and rest frequently, breathing heavily and complaining about how much her joints ached. She also often put her hands down her pants in an apparent act of self-soothing, much to others' dismay. Patricia was hospitalized due to repeated suicidal ideations and erratic behaviors. After getting to know her, I learned that in addition to her regular meals, she would consume up to 8 two-liter sodas and as many bags of chips or Cheetos as she could get her hands on throughout the day. The dietitians on staff tried to limit her access to junk food, but she had an uncanny knack for acquiring it.

When Patricia described her childhood, she described a life full of unrelenting chaos, violence, and abuse. She described eating at the kitchen counter while she listened to the sounds of her stepfather beating her mother. She told me she used to sneak back down to the kitchen after her older brother left the room after sexually abusing her each night and ate until she forgot what she had experienced and witnessed that day. In essence, from a very early age, food was the only thing she could count on to make her feel okay. Food had become the friend she could rely on and her calm within the emotional storm.

Most people's relationships with food, however unhealthy, are not as extreme as Patricia's, but the essence of her story is familiar to many of us. People who have been through extremely difficult life events or who are under chronic stress often use food as a way to self-soothe. For some this results in occasional binge eating, while for others it becomes a more chronic problem. The other extreme is to develop an overly controlled relationship with food in the aftermath of a traumatic event, such as engaging in extreme dieting, exercise, or caloric deprivation. Such overly controlled behaviors often serve as a means of feeling in control again after experiencing things that made them feel utterly helpless.

Another common phenomenon is that you might have trouble listening to your body's cues on hunger and fullness. You may find yourself waiting too long to eat and then becoming frantically hungry, and/or you have trouble discerning when you're full because you're eating mindlessly. Eating nourishing meals regularly and learning to tune in to your bodily cues will help you avoid blood sugar spikes or crashes and support your overall healing process.

Regular exercise is also critical to maintaining optimal health and well-being. Because trauma disrupts your body's natural equilibrium, freezes you in a state of hyperarousal and fear, and throws your nervous system out of balance, simply moving your body can be a crucial part of your healing. Exercise also helps you burn off the excess adrenaline you may have secreted due to an overactive stress response and encourages your body to release endorphins, which translate to positive emotional states. Exercise can help you feel stronger, more empowered, and reconnected with your body.

Ideally, try to exercise for at least thirty minutes per day. If it is easier for you, aim for smaller spurts of exercise throughout the day while still aiming to reach at least thirty minutes total. As you exercise, try to do so mindfully. Instead of zoning out or getting lost in your thoughts, see if you can focus on the physical sensations of the movement. Notice how you feel after you exercise. You will often find that you have more energy and feel like you are in a more positive and hopeful mental state.

Your Story, Part Three: What Is Your Body Telling You?

Instructions: Continue to write your story in the space provided below. This time, try to tune in to what your body is telling you. What changes have you noticed in your body after the trauma you experienced? Do you feel more sluggish or restless? Do you have areas of pain or tension in your body that you did not experience before? Do you experience pain or tension in any part or parts of your body that may have been directly affected by the trauma you endured? Have you gotten sick more easily since the trauma, or do you show any other signs that your immune system is compromised? Have you developed a new illness or disease since the trauma, or has an existing condition worsened?

Explore all the signs your body may be giving you, even if it does not immediately or directly seem relevant to the trauma you endured. Write freely and without judgment. Don't worry about your writing style, spelling, or grammar. Just let the words flow freely.

EXERCISE: SELF-CARE ASSESSMENT

Instructions: Use the following guide to determine how you are doing in these common areas of wellness and self-care. Once you identify areas for further growth, you can translate these areas into concrete goals.

	RARELY	SOMETIMES	REGULARLY
Emotional Wellness			
I regularly engage in activities that make me feel happy			
I find myself laughing often			
I try to catch and correct negative thinking patterns			
I feel good about myself			
Physical Wellness			
I try to eat healthy, regular meals			
I try to limit my intake of processed food and refined sugar			
I take vitamins and supplements			
I exercise for at least thirty minutes per day			
I drink sixty-four ounces of water each day			
Intellectual Wellness			
I engage in activities that involve pursuing and/or retaining knowledge			
I try to think critically about relevant political or social issues			
When I have a problem, I try to find solutions using a range of strategies and resources			
I have a sense of curiosity about the world around me			
Spiritual Wellness			
I have a set of beliefs or principles that give my life meaning or purpose			
I have faith in something beyond myself			
I engage in kind acts or service to others			
I am part of a religious or spiritual community			
Social Wellness and Sense of Community			
I have meaningful relationships			
I feel a sense of connectedness to others			
I am myself around other people			
I am friendly and supportive of others			

What values do you hold in regard to your physical health?

_____

_____

_____

Using the scale below, rate how important it is to you to engage in regular physical activity.

1	2	3	4	5	6	7	8	9	10
Not at all				Moderately					Very Important

Using the scale below, rate how important it is for you to feel strong.

1	2	3	4	5	6	7	8	9	10
Not at all				Moderately					Very Important

Using the scale below, rate how important it is for you to be pain free.

1	2	3	4	5	6	7	8	9	10
Not at all				Moderately					Very Important

Using the scale below, rate how important it is for you to feel flexible and relaxed.

1	2	3	4	5	6	7	8	9	10
Not at all				Moderately					Very Important

Exercise continues to next page

How closely does your current lifestyle match your values surrounding physical health?

....

....

....

What changes can you make to be living in a way that is more closely aligned with your values?

....

....

....

The Importance of Nutrition

The importance of good nutrition in stabilizing mood and managing mental health symptoms cannot be overstated. The field of *nutritional psychiatry* is based on the premise that the foods you eat directly affect your brain chemistry and, consequently, how you feel. For example, serotonin helps regulate sleep and mood and inhibits pain sensations. The majority of serotonin is produced in your gastrointestinal tract, so it makes sense that your digestive system influences your mood. Research has shown that more traditional diets, like the Mediterranean diet or a traditional Japanese diet, can yield up to 35 percent lower rates of depression when compared to a traditional Western diet, which typically includes a higher percentage of processed foods, fatty meats, and refined sugars. Increased stress can also directly compromise your ability to make healthy food decisions, as it has been shown to be associated with a greater preference for energy- and nutrient-dense foods, especially those that are high in sugar and fat. Under increased stress, most of us are more likely to choose pizza over fish, or potato chips over fruits and vegetables.

We've also learned that people who take probiotic supplements show reduced rates of anxiety and depression and less perceived stress. Increasing the amount of omega-3s someone consumes, either via a supplement or by increasing their consumption of omega-3-rich foods (such as salmon, chia seeds, sardines, and spinach) has also been found to be a potent antidepressant. Animal studies have also suggested that fish oil may be linked to hippocampal brain regeneration (known as *neurogenesis*), which is crucial in reducing the length of fear-dependent hippocampal memory. In a study of rescue workers following the Great East Japan Earthquake and tsunami that occurred in 2011, taking fish oil supplements reduced the severity of PTSD symptoms in female rescue workers. In other words, it's becoming increasingly clear that a nutritionally rich diet high in fruits, vegetables, and lean fats and low in processed foods and refined sugars is ideal for your overall mental health.

EXERCISE: FOOD JOURNAL

Keeping a food journal is an excellent way to assess your current nutritional and eating habits, especially if you have a tendency to engage in mindless eating (which translates to forgetting about that bag of chips you ate last night or the three cookies you had during a staff meeting, and/or overestimating how healthy your diet is). In 2011, the US Department of Agriculture replaced the food pyramid that many Americans grew up on with a new visual aid to guide healthy eating, "MyPlate." In response to the obesity epidemic, MyPlate reduces the emphasis on heavier foods and places more emphasis on eating greens and vegetables. Use the MyPlate visual to help aid your assessment of your diet throughout the week and to identify areas for improvement.

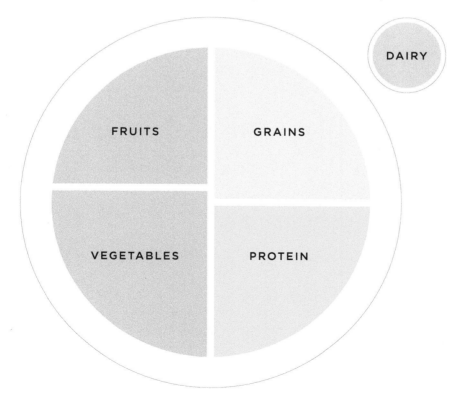

	MONDAY	TUESDAY	WEDNESDAY
Breakfast			
Lunch			
Dinner			
Supplements?			
Water Intake			
Note to self: *Use this space to note how well you aligned with the MyPlate recommendations or make other observations about your food intake (e.g., high in sugar, low in vegetables, included food rich in omega-3 fatty acids).*			

THURSDAY	FRIDAY	SATURDAY	SUNDAY

EXERCISE: MINDFUL EATING

How often do you really pay attention to your food while you are eating? Do you usually rush through eating? Or eat while you are on the go or watching television?

The following conscious eating meditation can help you become more mindful of your food and hunger levels.

1. As you sit in front of your food, take a few deep breaths. Notice your hunger cues. Are you starving or mildly hungry?
2. Observe your food. Notice the food's color, shape and texture. Does the food look appealing to you? Do you notice any physical sensations, like slight salivation?
3. Begin to take your first bite. As the food nears your mouth, take a moment to notice any smells. Again, do you notice any physical sensations?
4. When you begin to chew your food, move slowly. Notice the texture and temperature of the food in your mouth. Notice the various tastes you encounter. Begin to label the various tastes and sensations in your mind (e.g., "I notice the sweetness of the orange," or "I notice the crunch of the lettuce"). Chew your food for longer than you do typically.
5. When you swallow, notice the sensations in your mouth and throat. Notice your stomach. Can you feel the food reach your stomach? What hunger sensations are you experiencing? Does your stomach still feel empty, or is it beginning to fill?
6. As you continue to eat your food, try to stay mindful of your sensations. Take a breath between bites. As with other meditations, when your mind wanders, gently bring it back to your experience of eating.

EXERCISE: FOOD AND NUTRITION VALUES WORKSHEET

What values do you hold in regard to your food and nutrition?

....

....

....

Using the scale below, rate how important it is to you to eat healthy, nourishing foods.

1	2	3	4	5	6	7	8	9	10
Not at all				Moderately					Very Important

Using the scale below, rate how important it is for you to eat regular meals.

1	2	3	4	5	6	7	8	9	10

Not at all   Moderately   Very Important

Using the scale below, rate how important it is for you to limit your intake of refined sugar or processed foods.

1	2	3	4	5	6	7	8	9	10

Not at all   Moderately   Very Important

Using the scale below, rate how much you believe the food you eat impacts your overall health and wellness.

1	2	3	4	5	6	7	8	9	10

Not at all   Moderately   Very Important

How closely does your current lifestyle match your values surrounding food and nutrition?

What changes can you make to be living in a way that is more closely aligned with your values?

Chapter Takeaways

Trauma impacts your entire being: mind, brain, and body. Because of this, your journey toward healing needs to include strategies that care for your physical well-being. In this chapter you learned:

- How chronic stress can wreak havoc on your physical body and lead to physical pain and other illnesses.
- How to take steps to learn to relax and more effectively manage stress.
- How relaxation and stress reduction strategies will help you avoid unnecessary pain and illness for years to come.
- How each step you take to form a new health habit, whether it is related to getting better sleep, feeling more connected to your body, eating better, or engaging in more physical activity, will give you more strength, confidence, and mental acuity to help you face life's challenges.

CHAPTER 5

Your Relationships

What You'll Learn in This Chapter

In this chapter you will learn about how trauma can impact your relationships with yourself and others, leading to feelings of isolation and loneliness or a general sense of disconnection. After a traumatic event it can feel safest to avoid human contact as a way of mitigating risk or harm. However, we're going to discuss how important it is to rebuild connections to the people who are important to you and stop avoiding relationships and emotional intimacy. Emotional intimacy and human contact are critical supports on your path to wellness.

You'll also learn about how your brain and body attempt to protect you from the overwhelming emotional and physical pain of a traumatic experience with two processes called *fragmentation* and *dissociation*. While initially protective in the immediate aftermath of trauma, fragmentation can lead to disconnection and splits in your personality, behaviors, and sense of self. In order to heal from fragmentation, you will eventually need to embrace all parts of yourself and your experiences with a sense of compassion and nurturing.

Trauma, Isolation, and Alienation

After living through something so difficult, it's common to feel isolated both emotionally and physically. You may be thinking that no one can really understand what you went through, which likely leaves you feeling misunderstood and alone. Some survivors rarely talk about what happened to them—or never talk about it at all, which only intensifies feelings of isolation. You may be surrounded by people and appear to have "good" relationships in your life, but if you never share what's really going on, you'll eventually be left feeling disconnected. Some trauma survivors may even end relationships with the people in their lives who know about what happened, in a misguided effort to forget or to block out all reminders of trauma.

The problem with these strategies is that human beings have an innate need to connect with others. Because of this, you may experience an internal conflict in which part of you desperately craves connection, while another part wants to escape to the safety of solitude. I've worked with many clients who found it easier to engage in superficial relationships rather than maintain the relationships with people they were once truly close to. It's also common for a survivor to think they want a romantic relationship and fall in love quickly and easily, only to find themselves sabotaging the new relationship out of fear.

The process of truly reconnecting with other people will take work and some emotional risk on your part. It can feel so much easier to remain isolated in the places and spaces where you feel safe. You will likely need to encourage yourself to be around other people and, more importantly, to be real with them, which means being at least a little bit open about what you're going through. While the risk of rejection and hurt will always be a scary part of being in relationships, the benefits of social and emotional support and connection are critical to healing fully and something we're all hardwired to need in our lives.

Self-Alienation

In addition to feeling alone and isolated from others, you may also notice a painful disconnection from certain aspects of yourself. As we've talked about elsewhere, the brain and body attempt to protect you from the overwhelming experience of the traumatic event. During a trauma, a disconnection between the right and left hemispheres of the brain sometimes occurs. This not only leads to fragmented memories of what happened to you, but it can also lead to fragmentations in your personality and behaviors as you begin to heal.

The logical left side of your brain may successfully maintain its focus on the tasks of daily living, allowing you to stay in your job and make it through your day-to-day routine. However, the more experiential right side of your brain, where the majority of your trauma memories are stored, may remain in a continued state of fear, vulnerability, or shame. You may attempt to ignore this part of you in favor of just getting through your day, which is certainly understandable but unfortunately leads to further fragmentation and self-alienation. You may also judge these traumatized emotional responses in yourself as negative or weak, thus attempting to further distance yourself from your experiences and labeling them as "not the real me." Unfortunately, disowning parts of yourself will only lead to feeling more unsafe and unsettled within your own skin.

How will you know if you're experiencing self-alienation? It can be especially hard to identify if you are good at suppressing the more painful aspects of your experiences. One sign of self-alienation is behaving very differently in different environments. For instance, if you're maintaining a successful sense of self and are functioning in your workplace but are miserable at home and having significant conflict or dysfunction in personal relationships, this may be a sign that you're alienated from certain parts of your experience. The two environments—work and home—are triggering different aspects of your trauma experience and eliciting different parts of your self that need to be reintegrated.

Other clues that you may be experiencing self-alienation are found in conflicting thoughts, beliefs, and behaviors. For instance, you may acknowledge a fear of abandonment (from the part of you that is seeking attachment) while at the same time engaging in behaviors that push away anyone who tries to get close to you, likely activated by the part that's on high alert for risk of vulnerability or hurt. Similarly, you may experience intense fear in relation to one of your trauma triggers (e.g., authority figures) while feeling numb to or disregarding real threats to your safety (e.g., engaging in reckless driving or risky substance use). Some survivors who are experiencing self-alienation describe a vague sense of "faking it" or feeling like observers, as opposed to participants, in their lives.

To begin healing self-alienation, try to remain open to all aspects of your experiences and respond to yourself and your emotions with unconditional compassion. What are your thoughts and emotions trying to tell you? Each step in understanding yourself is a step toward regaining a sense of wholeness and authenticity.

EXERCISE: PRACTICING ACTS OF SELF-COMPASSION

Taking time to be kind to ourselves and engaging in activities that bring pleasure to our lives is very important in working toward healing and living a full, rich life.

EXAMPLES OF ACTIVITIES THAT PROVIDE SELF-NURTURING

Instructions: Put a check mark next to activities that you already engage in.
  Circle or underline activities that you would like to add to your life.

☐ Spend time in nature

☐ Take a walk

☐ Read a book

☐ Watch movies

☐ Take a warm bath

☐ Attend a religious service

☐ Post encouraging notes or positive statements around my home

☐ Listen to music

☐ Exercise

☐ Meditate

☐ Practice yoga

☐ Cook or bake

☐ Write or read a poem

☐ Travel or go on a short local getaway

☐ Learn something new

☐ Play with a pet

☐ Swim

☐ Dance

☐ Play with children

☐ Visit a museum or gallery

☐ Go out to eat

☐ Make yourself a nice meal

☐ Engage in a craft or hobby

☐ Create a home spa day

☐ Play sports

☐ Volunteer

☐ Go to a concert

☐ Go to a comedy club

☐ Go to an interesting lecture

☐ Go to the library

☐ Read a magazine

☐ Watch a favorite television show

☐ Make art

☐ Go to a coffee shop

☐ Improve an area of your home

☐ Play cards

☐ Play a game

☐ _____

☐ _____

☐ _____

IDEALLY, TRY TO ENGAGE IN A SELF-NURTURING ACTIVITY EVERY DAY.

To begin, pick at least three self-nurturing activities that you can commit to engaging in over the coming week. To hold yourself accountable, check off the activity after you do it.

1. _____ ☐

2. _____ ☐

3. _____ ☐

Rebuilding Your Relationship with Yourself

Feeling disconnected from yourself is a common experience in the aftermath of trauma. Especially if you experience (or have experienced) intrusive memories and flashbacks or persistent negative thoughts, your own mind and body can become a scary place to be. In the same way you might take steps to reconnect with an old friend, there are steps you can take to begin rebuilding your relationship with yourself.

Be curious. When you experience a difficult thought, memory, or emotion, your first instinct may be to distance yourself from it. Try to stay present and approach your experiences with a sense of curiosity, just as you would approach someone you were trying to get to know better. What are your emotions and thoughts trying to tell you? Where are these thoughts and feelings coming from? What experiences are these thoughts and feelings tied to? What behaviors or urges do these thoughts and feelings encourage you to engage in? Is the behavior urge related to an automatic trauma response or something that's in line with your current goals or values?

Be kind. Be kind to yourself. The more you can begin to accept all aspects of yourself, the safer and calmer your internal world will become.

Try not to judge your emotions or thoughts as they arise. You can acknowledge the difference between a helpful or harmful thought or a difficult versus pleasant emotion without judging yourself for having it. Be mindful of your internal critic. When you notice you're saying harmful things to yourself, pause and observe what is coming up for you. Try to shift your internal dialogue to a more compassionate one, without spending time or energy judging or reprimanding yourself for your initial thoughts.

Reconnect with your body. You can also take time to reconnect with your body and physical sensations. Yoga can be particularly useful in this endeavor, as there are aspects of the practice designed specifically to reconnect mind and body, breath and movement. Any form of exercise or movement can help you reconnect with your body as long as you remain present during the experience as opposed to letting your mind wander. As you move your body, notice the physical sensations that arise. Notice where you hold tension in your body and try to release it through your movements. Notice where you feel strong or supported in your body. Try to cultivate an attitude of appreciation for the body you live in.

Your Family and Friends

In the wake of trauma, you will likely find you have some difficulty trusting others, feeling close to people, or communicating effectively. You may feel numb or distant from others or feel intensely protective of those you love, causing you to become tense or anxious around them. Furthermore, if you're dealing with intrusive memories or flashbacks, you may be avoiding certain people, activities, and places in order to avoid getting triggered. Simply managing your symptoms may take so much of your mental time and energy that you have little left to focus on other people. This will all impact your relationships with your friends and family.

What can you do to begin reconnecting with your loved ones? Most importantly, share at least a little bit of what is going on with you. Many trauma survivors are hesitant to share their internal struggles for fear of burdening those around them. You don't have to go into great detail, but share something about what you're going through to provide loved ones with more context for your posttrauma behavior and opportunities to help support you. After a traumatic event, you may feel hypersensitive to criticism or rejection. Try to be aware of when your reaction to others has more to do with your internal struggles or triggers than with the other person's intentions toward you. Give your loved ones the benefit of the doubt before reacting. At the same time, do not tolerate abusive behavior from people in your life. Be aware of when you're continuing patterns of abuse in your relationships because the familiar pain or distress can feel safer.

Isolation, Avoidance, and Your Social Life

It's not difficult to understand how PTSD and other trauma-related symptoms can lead to isolation and avoidance. Symptoms of hyperarousal (i.e., feeling on guard, startling easily, or having difficulty concentrating) can be exhausting, leaving you with little energy to engage in social activities. You may be avoiding certain people or situations for fear of being triggered. Alternatively, if you do get out and socialize, you may feel distracted or embarrassed by your behavior or reactions when you're engaging with your friends or in public. On top of that, your efforts to avoid extremely painful emotions may have contributed to a constricted emotional range, which can make you feel numb to pleasurable emotions or make it difficult for you to find pleasure in activities you once enjoyed.

Unfortunately, while you may feel that you're avoiding potential pain by isolating, isolation is typically associated with more extreme and long-lasting trauma-related symptoms, worsening fear of the outside world, increasing feelings of loneliness, and lowering self-esteem. Over time, isolating will just make it scarier to go out and do things. You may also experience a shrinking in your friends network as people start to take the hint that you're not keen on socializing.

For many people looking to rebuild social connections, it can feel safer to start with people who've also been through a traumatic event, especially if you are feeling misunderstood by or different from those around you. Finding a trauma support group can be a great place to start, and the exercises that follow are designed to help you seek the support you need to stay on the road to recovery. (Refer to the Resources section of this workbook, starting on page 135, for help getting started with this search.)

EXERCISE: ASKING FOR HELP

Asking for help can be hard for everyone. However, there are probably many people in your life who would love to be helpful to you but may not know exactly how. Being clear on what you want from people will help you take the first step toward asking for that help. Asking for help is one of the best ways to get the support that you want and deserve.

Who I am asking for help: _____

What would be helpful for this person to do (or say) to support me in my recovery?

_____

_____

_____

What is not helpful for this person to do (or say) to support me in my recovery?

_____

_____

_____

How and when am I going to ask for help?

_____

_____

_____

EXERCISE: IDENTIFY YOUR AVOIDANCE BEHAVIORS

Instructions: Use the following worksheet to begin to identify what you are avoiding in regard to your social life and relationships.

PEOPLE AND PLACES:

Are there any specific people (or types of people) or places (or types of places) that you have been avoiding since your traumatic experience? List below:

ACTIVITIES:

Are there any social activities that you used to enjoy that you have been avoiding since your traumatic experience? List below:

EMOTIONAL AVOIDANCE:

What emotional experiences have you been avoiding (or engaging in less) since your traumatic experience? Examples include sharing your true thoughts and feelings, talking to people about what happened to you, and getting emotionally close to someone. List below:

EXERCISE: VALUES WORKSHEET: WHAT DO YOU WANT TO CHANGE?

Instructions: Use the following worksheet to identify any differences between your current level of social and relationship engagement and where you want to be.

How often do you see people you care about each week?

0	1	2	3	4	5	6	7
Never/Rarely		A Few Times		Most Days		Almost Daily/Daily	

How often do you want to see people you care about each week?

0	1	2	3	4	5	6	7
Never/Rarely		A Few Times		Most Days		Almost Daily/Daily	

How often do you talk to people you care about each week?

0	1	2	3	4	5	6	7
Never/Rarely		A Few Times		Most Days		Almost Daily/Daily	

How often do you want to talk to people you care about each week?

0	1	2	3	4	5	6	7
Never/Rarely		A Few Times		Most Days		Almost Daily/Daily	

How often do you engage in social activities each week?

0	1	2	3	4	5	6	7
Never/Rarely		A Few Times		Most Days		Almost Daily/Daily	

How often do you want to engage in social activities each week?

0	1	2	3	4	5	6	7
Never/Rarely		A Few Times		Most Days		Almost Daily/Daily	

How often are you open with people about what you are going through each week?

0	1	2	3	4	5	6	7
Never/Rarely		A Few Times		Most Days		Almost Daily/Daily	

How often do you want to be open with people about what you are going through each week?

0	1	2	3	4	5	6	7
Never/Rarely		A Few Times		Most Days		Almost Daily/Daily	

EXERCISE: ALTERNATIVES TO AVOIDANCE

Instructions: Now that you have identified some of your avoidant behavior in regard to your social life and relationships, start to think about alternative behaviors. For this worksheet, don't worry about what you are actually willing to do, what is realistic, or what sounds too scary. Just brainstorm as many alternatives as you think of. For most avoidant behavior, the alternative action is simply to engage in the behavior instead of avoiding it.

AVOIDANT BEHAVIOR	ALTERNATIVE BEHAVIOR(S)

EXERCISE: RATING THE ALTERNATIVE BEHAVIORS

Instructions: Now that you have identified possible alternatives to your avoidant behaviors, list them in hierarchical order from the most scary or difficult (at the top of the mountain) down to the least (at the bottom of the mountain) with 0% being least difficult and 100% being most difficult.

ALTERNATIVE BEHAVIOR	DIFFICULTY RATING (0% TO 100%)

EXERCISE: YOUR PLAN FOR CHANGE

Instructions: Prior to completing your plan for change, you may want to review some of the worksheets you previously completed in this section for ideas about where to begin. For example, you may want to review the worksheets related to avoidant and alternative behaviors and the values worksheet related to what you want to change.

I want to make the following changes in regard to my social life and relationships:

The reasons why I want to make these changes are:

I plan to start making these changes by taking the following steps:

(If engaging in alternative behaviors, you may want to begin with some of the behaviors with lower difficulty ratings and work your way up.)

Exercise continues to next page

The people in my life can help me make these changes by (ideally, take this a step further and ask these people for the help you need):

....

....

....

....

What could get in the way of making these changes?

....

....

....

How will I overcome these barriers?

....

....

....

Isolation and Intimacy

As we've been discussing, feeling isolated is more than just physically staying away from people; it also refers to emotional isolation or a lack of intimacy. Although often associated with romantic relationships, intimacy can be cultivated in any of your important relationships. Intimacy involves feeling a sense of closeness or familiarity with another person as well as affection and warmth toward that person—whether it's a close friend, a romantic partner, or a family member. Intimacy can also be characterized by a sense of confidence and trust in the other person.

This typically develops from spending a lot of time with one another, sharing life experiences, and mutually sharing emotional experiences. You may notice that the people you feel most comfortable confiding in are the same people who have confided in you about *their* lives. This is because the reciprocal act of sharing honest emotional experiences with other people and being received with compassion and understanding is one of foundations of an intimate bond.

After a traumatic event it can be more difficult to experience intimacy in your relationships. As you begin to crave more intimacy in your relationships, start by taking small steps toward reconnecting with the people in your life. You may want to start with the person or people you trust the most. For many people, this person may be someone they've known for a long time, but for others this may not be the case. However, you do not want to rely solely on strangers or acquaintances for support (with the exception of a mental health professional or a structured support setting, like a support group). You'll have more difficulty accurately anticipating the reactions of people you do not know well, which could inadvertently reinforce or exacerbate your difficulties trusting others.

Trauma, Healing, and Sexuality

Sexuality can be a particularly scary or painful area for survivors of trauma, especially for survivors of sexual assault, rape, or sexual exploitation. Even for individuals who experienced a trauma that didn't involve sex, sexuality can still be triggering because it requires us to be so vulnerable.

Many survivors experience extreme ambivalence toward sexuality, simultaneously wanting to engage in sexual intimacy and recoiling at the first sign of physical contact. For survivors of sexual assault, sexuality is often shrouded in shame and confusion, especially if they experienced a biologically natural pleasure reaction, despite the act being otherwise offensive and unwanted. It's also common for trauma survivors to engage in frequent promiscuous or unsafe sex due to a deep need for intimacy, familiarity, or power. Sometimes survivors find that sexual acts no longer feel intimate or special to them, or they use them as a way to numb or avoid other emotional experiences.

Use these strategies to help you begin to reclaim a healthy sexual life:

Create opportunities to experience nonthreatening sensuality. Research has demonstrated a clear association between childhood or adolescent sexual abuse and later sexual dysfunction; however, this association is lessened if the individual also has positive experiences with touch, trust, and empathy as well as the ability to relax and be soothed. This suggests that one of the pathways to healing is engaging in nonsexual experiences related to touch, trust, and relaxation, such as massage therapy (or other forms of bodywork) or yoga. Other ways to experience nonthreatening sensuality include listening to sensual music, lighting a candle, applying scented lotion, or watching or reading about romantic sex scenes in movies or books.

Define your goals and boundaries around sex. Before you engage in sexual acts, think clearly about what you want and do not want. For instance, you may have a goal related to starting to date or enjoy sex again. It is just as important to be clear ahead of time about what you do not want. For instance, you may decide that you do not want to kiss anyone on a first date or that you're not ready to engage in oral sex. Your goals and boundaries can change over time, but being clear about what you want will help you feel more in control of your sex life. If you're in a committed relationship, it will be important to communicate your goals and boundaries around sex with your partner.

Instructions: Write the names of the people who are most important to you in circles below. The circles closest to you represent the people you trust the most and who are the most important to you (moving outward).

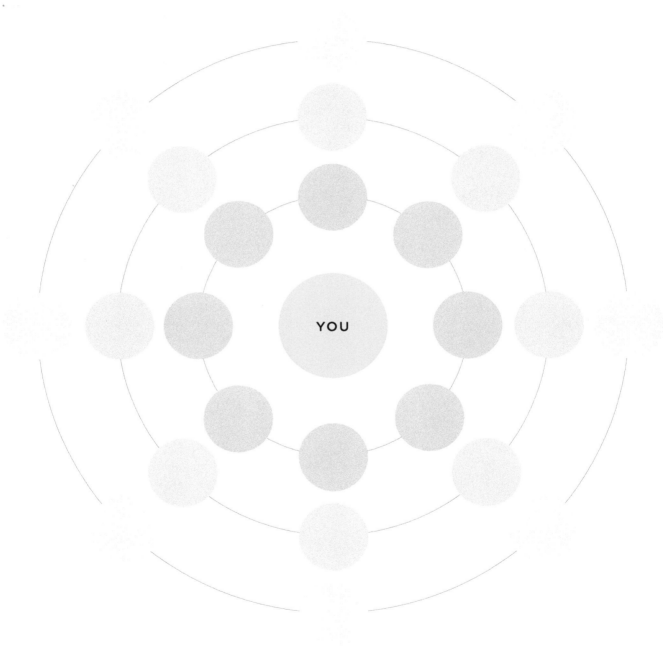

Instructions: Use the following worksheet to reflect upon how trauma has impacted your close relationships. To repeat the exercise with multiple close relationships, you can either photocopy the worksheet or simply write the answers to the same questions on a separate sheet of paper.

How has trauma impacted my relationship with _____*?*

1. Do I see this person more or less since the traumatic event?

   ☐ More   ☐ Less   ☐ No Change

   Thoughts about the change:

   _____

   _____

2. Since the trauma, am I more or less comfortable around this person?

   ☐ More   ☐ Less   ☐ No Change

   Thoughts about the change:

   _____

   _____

3. Since the trauma, am I more or less honest and open with this person?

   ☐ More   ☐ Less   ☐ No Change

   Thoughts about the change:

   _____

   _____

EXERCISE: RELATIONSHIP VALUES: WHAT DO I WANT?

Instructions: Use the following writing prompts to reflect upon what types of relationships you want to have and who you want to be within your relationships.

FAMILY RELATIONSHIPS:

What types of relationships do I want to have with my family?

_____

_____

_____

Pick one of your family roles (i.e., son, sister, nephew, etc.) and reflect upon what type of family member you want to be in that role:

_____

_____

_____

MARRIAGE/COUPLES/ROMANTIC RELATIONSHIPS:

What type of relationships do you want?

_____

_____

_____

What type of partner do you want to be?

_____

_____

_____

PARENTING:

What do you want your relationship with your child (or children) to look like?

_____

_____

_____

What type of parent do you want to be?

_____

_____

_____

FRIENDSHIPS:

What do you want your friendships to be like?

_____

_____

_____

What type of friend do you want to be?

....

....

....

EXERCISE: SHIFTING HARSH SELF-TALK
TO COMPASSIONATE SELF-TALK

We're often much harder on ourselves than we would be on someone we love or a small child. When you catch yourself engaging in harsh self-talk, take a moment and think about how you would talk to someone else in the same situation (such as a close friend or a toddler). After you have identified a more compassionate way of speaking, use that same compassionate statement with yourself. Continue to work on catching and shifting your harsh self-talk until more compassionate self-talk becomes habitual.

Examples of harsh self-talk include statements such as:

"I'm worthless."
"I'm a loser."
"I can't do anything right."
"It was all my fault."
"I'm such an idiot."

HARSH SELF-TALK	COMPASSIONATE SELF-TALK
(Would you say the same thing to someone you love or to a small child?)	(What would you say to someone you love or to a small child?)

EXERCISE: LOVING-KINDNESS MEDITATION

Instructions: Traditionally, loving-kindness meditations begin with a focus on the self and then on someone you love. Next, you shift your focus to someone you have had difficult interactions with, and then end with a focus on all beings. When you feel *really* ready, the "difficult person" could be the perpetrator of the trauma you experienced. But to start, choose a difficult person who is less triggering.

1. Begin in a comfortable seated position.
2. Close your eyes if you are comfortable doing so (and if you have sufficiently memorized the below verses).
3. Place your hand on your heart and take a deep breath in and out.
4. Maintain your hand placement and deep breathing as you recite the following verses (or verses with a similar intention) out loud or to yourself:
   » May I be free from suffering.
   » May I experience pure joy.
   » May I be at peace.
   » May [someone you love] be free from suffering.
   » May [someone you love] experience pure joy.
   » May [someone you love] be at peace.
   » May [a person you have had difficult interactions with] be free from suffering.
   » May [a person you have had difficult interactions with] experience pure joy.
   » May [a person you have had difficult interactions with] be at peace.
   » May all beings be free from suffering.
   » May all beings experience pure joy.
   » May all beings be at peace.

Chapter Takeaways

In this chapter we discussed how trauma commonly impacts survivors' relationships with themselves and others, and you were encouraged to reflect on how trauma has impacted your own relationships.

After reading this chapter you should have a sense of:

- How trauma has changed your relationship with yourself.
- How trauma has impacted your relationships with important people in your life.
- Avoidant behaviors in which you may be engaging that are limiting your ability to connect to others.
- A better sense of what you want out of your relationships.
- Tools you can use to rebuild a healthy relationship with sexuality.
- Steps you can take to regain a sense of connection with others and to regain a sense of intimacy in your relationships.
- Steps you can take to rebuild your relationship with yourself.

CHAPTER 6

The Road Ahead

What You'll Learn in This Chapter

In many ways, you'll be living with the effects of the trauma you endured for the rest of your life. But this need not stop you from leading a full, balanced, fulfilling, and happy life. Think of this workbook as a long-term resource that you can return to anytime you start to struggle. You may even return to some of the exercises or sections of this workbook for a refresher or periodic "tune-up" when things are going well, to help you stay on track. In this final chapter, we'll talk about how you can stay on the path to recovery.

Long-Term Outlook

Because of the enormity of what you endured, there is no quick fix or pill you can take to recover from the trauma you experienced. Many of the strategies we've discussed so far are meant to facilitate long-term lifestyle shifts in the ways you manage any remaining symptoms, handle difficult thoughts and emotions, and apply positive, self-nurturing strategies like self-compassion, healthy body practices, and healthy relationship and intimacy practices.

Taking care of yourself is a lifelong job. Now that you've identified your triggers, signs of serious stress, and your trauma-related symptoms, you'll need to maintain awareness of them *even if they seem to have resolved*. It's not uncommon for signs of acute stress or trauma-related symptoms to resurface after going quiet for some time, especially if you're confronted with a new life stressor, like the death of a loved one or the loss of a job. Ideally you will have developed a good sense of what you are like and how you feel when you are doing well, so that you can catch any signs of difficulty and intervene early before you return to less healthy habits or old, ineffective ways of managing your symptoms.

While it can seem like a lot of work to maintain balance and health, it's typically easier to maintain healthy habits and mental health gains than it is to start all over again if you experience a full return of your trauma-related symptoms or unhealthy patterns. You deserve all the effort that it takes to feel good and to live the life you want.

Your Biggest Challenges So Far

You have likely faced many challenges on your road to recovery. Some days just getting out of bed and facing the day may have felt like a challenge. It's easy to respond to these challenges in ways that make things worse, like engaging in catastrophic thinking, taking your frustration out on a loved one, or avoiding a problem by drinking alcohol. Hopefully this book has helped you start to learn strategies for responding to challenges in ways that are healthier and more effective. Take a minute now to reflect on which were the biggest challenges you faced along your path to healing.

EXERCISE: WHAT I HAVE LEARNED FROM MY BIGGEST CHALLENGES

Instructions: Reflect upon the biggest challenges you have faced thus far. What were they? What did you do to try to overcome those challenges? What worked? What could you have done better? What lessons can you take away from these experiences?

Your Biggest Victories So Far

Along with the many challenges you have faced, you have likely had many victories along your journey toward healing yourself. Celebrate those victories, both large and small. You've endured something that may have once been unimaginable to you—and you survived. You may have even grown into a stronger, more compassionate version of yourself. Try not to compare yourself to the person you were before the trauma or compare your life now to the one you had before. You cannot erase what happened to you, and you will never be exactly the same as you were. But you can celebrate who you are now and how far you've come.

EXERCISE: WHAT I HAVE LEARNED FROM MY BIGGEST VICTORIES

Instructions: Reflect upon your biggest victories. What were they? How did you get there? What lessons can you take away from these experiences?

Setting SMART Goals

Setting goals for yourself and your life can be a helpful tool for moving forward and continuing to evolve. Learning how to set the right kinds of goals can help you maximize your chance for success. Adhering to the following guidelines (based on the acronym *SMART*) will help you make the most of your goal setting.

Make sure your goal is:

Specific. Your goal should be clearly written and define exactly what you want to accomplish. If you set vague goals, like "wanting to feel better," you will have a difficult time knowing how, if, and when you reach it.

Measurable. You also want to set a goal that is measurable. How will you know when you have reached your goal? Try connecting your goal to a rating scale or amount of time, such as hours or days per week. For example, you may want

to reduce your overall feeling of sadness from a level 9 to a level 5 (on a scale of 1 to 10). Or you may want to increase the number of times you socialize or exercise per week.

Attainable. The goal must be something you can attain, taking into consideration your time and resources.

Reasonable. If you set an unreasonable goal, you will become easily discouraged. Start small and work your way toward the long-term change you want.

Time-limited. Setting a specific amount of time in which to accomplish your goal ensures that you take the time to check in with your progress. If you made progress toward your goal but didn't fully accomplish it, you may decide to continue working on the same goal within a new time frame.

The Road to Progress Isn't Always Straight

Sometimes you may feel like you've taken three steps forward only to take five steps back. Life can be unpredictable, and despite your best efforts, the road to recovery never runs in a straight line. As you work toward reducing a specific symptom or unhealthy behavior, you may notice that you have substituted one problem for another. For example, you may have worked tirelessly to control your anger only to find that you're left with intense feelings of sadness that you didn't experience before. Similarly, you may have finally stopped drinking in excess only to notice that you've developed a tendency to overeat. Sometimes alleviating one issue merely clears the way for another to surface.

All of that is to be expected, and if such things happen, try to recognize them as part of the normal healing process. Notice any patterns that run through difficulties like these, and try to identify the core issues or unresolved areas of pain that might be at work with these seemingly unrelated symptoms and behaviors.

Symptoms can also reappear even after you thought they were fully resolved. For example, after consistent work processing your trauma and reducing your avoidant behaviors, you may have experienced total relief from your trauma-related flashbacks only to experience an unexpected flashback much later that may have been triggered by something you were not even aware of. Periodic resurgence of symptoms is normal and does not necessarily indicate that you will return to your baseline or have to start all over. The important thing is that you keep moving forward, even if you feel frustrated at times. As you begin to accumulate more tools and strategies that work for you, you'll notice that you can apply many of the same principles and techniques to various problems or symptoms. Never underestimate all that you have already accomplished and what you can learn from the progress you've already made.

Building Your New Habits

Building habits that will help you thrive is critical in helping your forward momentum. Start with building basic lifestyle habits and routines that will make you less vulnerable to distress and emotional and behavioral dysregulation. These habits include ensuring that you get sufficient sleep, eat nutritious meals, exercise regularly, engage in enjoyable activities, and attend to your physical health via regular medical checkups.

These basic healthy habits will help you build the resources to continue to tackle life's inevitable stressors. It can be helpful to track your progress initially in order to stay on track. When maintaining a habit no longer requires a great deal of effort or mental energy, you have probably reached the stage of change in which the habit is likely to remain with you for a lifetime.

EXERCISE: WHAT I'M LIKE WHEN I'M DOING WELL

Instructions: Take a moment to think about what you are like when you are doing your best. This will help give you a reference point for the future in order to help you catch any signs that you are beginning to struggle. You can also use it to remind yourself of what it is like to be in a good place in your mind and life if you experience a resurgence of trauma-related symptoms that were once resolved.

What I feel like when I am doing well:

Exercise continues to next page

What are my habits and routines when I am doing well (e.g., how much do I sleep or exercise)?

_____

_____

_____

How much do I socialize, and whom do I feel connected with when I am doing well?

_____

_____

_____

What are my trauma-related symptoms like when I am doing well?

_____

_____

_____

Watch Out for Red Flags

Keep an eye out for any warning signs that you may be struggling or experiencing increased stress, which could lead to a resurgence of previously resolved trauma-related symptoms or exacerbate whatever remaining symptoms you may have. What are the signs that you are experiencing increased stress? Are you feeling irritable more frequently or having more difficulty sleeping? Do you find yourself feeling anxious for no reason or having increased difficulty concentrating? The more you can learn to catch the subtle signs of increasing stress, the more quickly you can intervene by engaging in healthy, stress-reducing activities like getting rest, reaching out to a loved one, or exercising.

You'll also need to keep an eye out for more serious red flags that may signal an uptick in trauma-related symptoms. These could include beginning to withdraw from your friends and family, experiencing increased trauma-related nightmares or intrusive thoughts, returning to unhelpful thought patterns, or feeling overwhelmed by painful emotions. When you notice these concerning shifts, you may need to take significant actions to return to an optimal level of functioning. Review the exercises and tools for healing contained in this workbook and engage in the strategies that worked for you before. You will also likely need to reach out to your support network, whether that's a loved one, a support group, or a professional therapist. The sooner you take action, the more quickly you'll find relief and get back on track.

EXERCISE: IDENTIFYING YOUR WARNING SIGNS

Instructions: The more aware you are of your personal red flags and warning signals, the faster you'll catch signs of increased stress, unhealthy habits that may be creeping back, and signs that your trauma-related symptoms may be worsening or returning. The more quickly you identify these warning signs, the sooner and more effectively you can take action.

What are the signs that you are experiencing increased stress or returning to unhealthy behaviors? What are your action plans related to these warning signs?

WARNING SIGN	ACTION PLAN

What are the signs that you are experiencing increased trauma-related symptoms? What are your action plans related to these warning signs?

WARNING SIGN	ACTION PLAN

Keep Writing Your New Story

At this point you've written, and then rewritten, the story of your trauma. While this experience will always be a part of you, you are in control of the next chapter of your life. Continue to reflect on your experiences in a way that helps move you forward, as opposed to getting stuck in a loop of painful thoughts or emotions. The trauma you endured has likely forced you to reconsider many of your beliefs about yourself and the world. Take that as an opportunity to focus on what's important to you and what you want your future to look like.

You now have the skills and ability to author this next chapter of your story in the way that is most meaningful to you. If you don't like where you're headed, sit down and rewrite your story.

EXERCISE: HOW HAVE YOU GROWN?

Although trauma brings a lot of heartache, it also presents you with opportunities for self-examination and growth. Use the following writing prompts to think about how you have grown and what you've learned from the trauma you experienced.

After the trauma you endured, have any of your priorities changed? Are there things in your life that you now appreciate more than you may have before? Elaborate below.

Have any of your spiritual beliefs changed since you experienced the traumatic event? Have any of your beliefs about the meaning of life or the purpose of your life changed? Elaborate below.

....

....

....

....

....

EXERCISE: WHAT I WANT TO WORK ON NEXT

Instructions: What goal are you working on now? Use the following worksheet to identify the primary short- and long-term goals that you want to focus on now. Your short-term goal should help you work toward your long-term goal. If possible, make your goals SMART, especially your short-term goal.

My next short-term goal:

....

....

....

Exercise continues to next page

The reason I want to work on this goal is:

....

....

....

This goal will help me reach my long-term goal, which is:

....

....

....

Find What Works for You

As you have gone through the exercises and tools in this workbook, you've likely found some strategies extremely helpful, while others may not have worked so well. It's fine to focus on the strategies that took you furthest fastest. Everyone's experience is different, and every journey to healing is unique. If you have difficulty identifying what works for you, think about a time when you were doing well and reflect on what strategies and behaviors you were engaging in at that time. As you continue moving forward, you may also notice that something that was once useful to you is no longer as helpful. Our needs shift over time, and our strategies and tools should, too. Be open to trying new things, even things that didn't work for you before. The more tools you have to work with, the more likely it is that you can overcome whatever obstacles you face.

Exercise: The Path Ahead: Setting Meaningful Goals

Instructions: Take a moment to think about the life that you want. What is important to you? Begin to set goals that will move you toward the life that you want to be living.

	VALUES What are your values related to this area of your life? What do you want this aspect of your life to look like?	GOAL Set a goal related to this area of your life that will help you move closer to the life you want to live.
Family		
Friends		
Work		
Learning		
Fun/Recreation		
Spirituality		
Health/Fitness/Wellness		
Community		
The Environment		
Beauty/Aesthetics/The Arts		
Other		

Building Your Support Network

Continue to build a network of support around you. This network can include your friends and family as well as structured forms of support like support groups (in person or online) and/or individual therapy (see the Resources section of this workbook for help finding structured and professional help).

Social connection is strongly correlated with both physical and mental health. Research also suggests that as we age, the importance of *quality* social connection becomes more important than the *quantity* of our social connections. Continue to cultivate more emotional support from within your existing network of friends, family, and loved ones. Asking for what you need and being open to receiving that support is a courageous act. You already know how to do hard things. Don't give up on the people around you, and, most importantly, don't ever give up on yourself.

Chapter Takeaways

In this chapter we reviewed how to continue along a long-term path to recovery and overall health. Specifically, we discussed:

- What you can learn from your biggest challenges and victories.
- How to manage setbacks and symptom resurgence.
- The importance of being aware of your personal "red flags" so you can get back on track quickly.
- How to set effective goals and track your progress.
- The importance of building a network of support.

As you look forward to the road ahead, remember that taking care of yourself will be a lifelong journey. When things get tough, remind yourself of how far you've come and all that you have accomplished. Continue to focus on building the life you want as you write your next chapter.

RESOURCES

Books:

The Complex PTSD Workbook: A Mind-Body Approach to Regaining Emotional Control and Becoming Whole by Arielle Schwartz, PhD (2017, Althea Press)

- This workbook is geared toward individuals with unresolved childhood trauma and includes education regarding the types of symptoms associated with early childhood trauma as well as tools to regain positive behaviors and beliefs.

Get out of Your Mind and into Your Life: The New Acceptance and Commitment Therapy by Steven C. Hayes, PhD (2005, New Harbinger Press)

- Guided by the evidence-based *Acceptance and Commitment Therapy*, this workbook encourages you to begin to embrace your life and your pain instead of fighting it.

Mind-Body Workbook for PTSD: A 10-Week Program for Healing after Trauma by Stanley H. Block, MD, and Carolyn Bryant Block (2010, New Harbinger Press)

- This workbook guides the reader through a ten-week program focused on techniques for reconnecting the mind and body.

The Posttraumatic Growth Workbook by Richard G. Tedeschi, PhD, and Bret A. Moore, PsyD, ABPP (2016, New Harbinger Publications)

- This workbook guides the reader to continue to focus on processing their trauma with an emphasis on gaining wisdom, strength, and resilience.

Websites:

International Society for Traumatic Stress Studies (ISTSS.org)

- Offers a function to search for trauma-informed therapists (ISTSS.org/find-a-clinician .aspx) as well as extensive resources related to understanding traumatic stress.

Mental Health America (MentalHealthAmerica.net)

- Offers many resources for your mental health including screening tools, a crisis line, and a support group search tool (MentalHealthAmerica.net/find-support-groups).

The National Child Traumatic Stress Network (NCTSN.org)

- Offers ample information related to understanding traumatic stress and effective treatment methods and includes links to various crisis lines.

National Suicide Prevention Lifeline (SuicidePreventionLifeline.org)

- Offers a 24/7 crisis line, with a chat option for individuals having suicidal thoughts. The website also provides information regarding suicide prevention and links to find your local help center.

Psychology Today (PsychologyToday.com)

- Offers many brief articles on various mental health topics as well as a national database of therapists and support groups (psychologytoday.com/us/groups/trauma-and-ptsd).

UCLA Mindful Awareness Research Center (MARC.UCLA.edu)

- Offers a library of free audio-guided meditations as well as other resources related to mindfulness.

The US Department of Veterans Affairs: National Center for PTSD (www.PTSD.va.gov)

- Offers resources for both veterans and civilians, including information regarding PTSD, crisis lines for veterans, and video testimonials from individuals who suffer from PTSD and their experiences with treatment.

REFERENCES

Boscarino, J. A. "Posttraumatic Stress Disorder and Physical Illness: Results from Clinical and Epidemiologic Studies." In *Biobehavioral Stress Response: Protective and Damaging Effects*, edited by R. Yehuda, B. McEwen, 141–153. New York: New York Academy of Sciences, 2004.

Briere, John, and Catherine Scott. *Principles of Trauma Therapy: A Guide to Symptoms, Evaluation, and Treatment*. Thousand Oaks, CA: Sage Publications, 2006.

Felitti, V. J., R. F. Anda, D. Nordenberg, D. F. Williamson, A. M. Spitz, V. Edwards, and J. S. Marks. "Relationship of Childhood Abuse and Household Dysfunction to Many of the Leading Causes of Death in Adults: The Adverse Childhood Experiences (ACE) Study." *American Journal of Preventive Medicine* 14(4) (May 1998): 245–258.

Fisher, J. *Healing the Fragmented Selves of Trauma Survivors: Overcoming Internal Self-Alienation*. New York: Routledge, Taylor and Francis Group, 2017.

Gupta, M. A. "Review of Somatic Symptoms in Post-traumatic Stress Disorder." *International Review of Psychiatry* 25(1) (February 2013): 86–99. https://doi.org/10.3109/09540261.2012.736367.

Ilardi, S. "Habits of Healthy Sleep." In *The Depression Cure*, 193–212. Cambridge, MA: Lifelong Books, 2009.

Kroenke, K., R. L. Spitzer, and J. B. W. Williams. "The PHQ-9: Validity of a Brief Depression Severity Measure." *Journal of General Internal Medicine* 16(9) (September 2001): 606–613. https://doi.org/10.1046/j.1525-1497.2001.016009606.x.

Lally, P., C. van Jaarsveld, H. Potts, and J. Wardle. "How Habits Are Formed: Modeling Habit Formation in the Real World." *Journal of European Social Psychology* 40 (October 2010): 998–1009.

Lee, S. Y., and C. L. Park. "Trauma Exposure, Posttraumatic Stress, and Preventive Health Behaviours: A Systematic Review." *Health Psychology Review* 12(1) (2018): 75–109. https://doi.org/10.1080/17437199.2017.1373030.

Lima, A., et al. "The Impact of Tonic Immobility Reaction on the Prognosis of Posttraumatic Stress Disorder." *Journal of Psychiatric Research* 44(4) (March 2010): 224–228.

Nishi, D., et. al. "Fish Oil for Attenuating Posttraumatic Stress Symptoms among Rescue Workers after the Great East Japan Earthquake: A Randomized Controlled Trial." *Psychotherapy and Psychosomatics* 81 (2012): 315–317. https://doi.org/10.1159/000336811.

Price, M., J. Spinazzola, R. Musicaro, J. Turner, M. Suvak, D. Emerson, and B. van der Kolk. "Effectiveness of an Extended Yoga Treatment for Women with Chronic Posttraumatic Stress Disorder." *The Journal of Alternative and Complementary Medicine* 23(4) (April 2017): 300–309. https://doi.org/10.1089/acm.2015.0266.

Rechtschaffen, A., and B. M. Bergmann. "Sleep Deprivation in the Rat: An Update of the 1989 Paper." *Sleep* 25(1) (February 2002): 18–24.

Resick, P. A., C. M. Monson, and K. M. Chard. *Cognitive Processing Therapy for PTSD: A Comprehensive Manual.* New York: Guilford Press, 2016.

Samuelson, K. W. "Post-traumatic Stress Disorder and Declarative Memory Functioning: A Review." *Dialogues in Clinical Neuroscience* 13(3) (September 2011): 346–351.

Sarris, J., et al. "Nutritional Medicine as Mainstream in Psychiatry." *Lancet Psychiatry* 2(3) (March 2015): 271–274. https://doi.org/10.1016/S2215-0366(14)00051-0.

Sperry, R. "Changing Priorities." *Annual Review of Neuroscience* 4 (1981): 1–16.

Tedeschi, R. G., and B. A. Moore. *The Posttraumatic Growth Workbook.* Oakland, CA: New Harbinger Publications, Inc., 2016.

Weir, E. "Drug-facilitated Date Rape." *CMAJ: Canadian Medical Association Journal* 165(1) (July 2001): 80.

INDEX

ABOUT THE AUTHOR

Elena Welsh, PhD, is a licensed clinical psychologist located in Los Angeles, California. Dr. Welsh received her doctorate degree from the University of Maryland, Baltimore County, and completed advanced clinical training through a postdoctoral fellowship at Gateways Psychiatric Hospital in Los Angeles. Dr. Welsh has worked with a wide range of clients who have experienced trauma, including survivors of torture, domestic violence, early childhood abuse, and sexual assault. She has published articles in various medical and research journals and has served as a consultant for statewide initiatives aimed at increasing trauma-informed care. Dr. Welsh also serves as an adjunct faculty member at Antioch University Los Angeles.

CPSIA information can be obtained
at www.ICGtesting.com
Printed in the USA
LVHW05s1651270918
591424LV00001B/1/P